At Issue

Should Drilling Be Allowed in the Arctic National Wildlife Refuge?

Other Books in the At Issue Series:

At Issue

Should Drilling Be Allowed in the Arctic National Wildlife Refuge?

Tamara Thompson, Book Editor

GREENHAVEN PRESS
A part of Gale, Cengage Learning

Detroit • New York • San Francisco • New Haven, Conn • Waterville, Maine • London

Elizabeth Des Chenes, *Director, Publishing Solutions*

© 2013 Greenhaven Press, a part of Gale, Cengage Learning

Gale and Greenhaven Press are registered trademarks used herein under license.

For more information, contact:
Greenhaven Press
27500 Drake Rd.
Farmington Hills, MI 48331-3535
Or you can visit our Internet site at http://www.gale.cengage.com

For product information and technology assistance, contact us at

Gale Customer Support, 1-800-877-4253

For permission to use material from this text or product, submit all requests online at www.cengage.com/permissions

Further permissions questions can be emailed to permissionrequest@cengage.com

Articles in Greenhaven Press anthologies are often edited for length to meet page requirements. In addition, original titles of these works are changed to clearly present the main thesis and to explicitly indicate the author's opinion. Every effort is made to ensure that Greenhaven Press accurately reflects the original intent of the authors. Every effort has been made to trace the owners of copyrighted material.

Cover image copyright © Debra Hughs 2007. Used under license from shutterstock.com.

LIBRARY OF CONGRESS CATALOGING-IN-PUBLICATION DATA

Should drilling be allowed in the Arctic National Wildlife Refuge? / Tamara Thompson, book editor.
    p. cm. -- (At issue)
    Includes bibliographical references and index.
    ISBN 978-0-7377-6199-3 (hardcover) -- ISBN 978-0-7377-6200-6 (pbk.)
    1. Oil well drilling--Environmental aspects--Alaska--Arctic National Wildlife Refuge. 2. Offshore oil well drilling--Environmental aspects--Alaska--Arctic National Wildlife Refuge. 3. Gas well drilling--Environmental aspects--Alaska--Arctic National Wildlife Refuge. 4. Offshore gas well drilling--Environmental aspects--Alaska--Arctic National Wildlife Refuge. 5. Petroleum reserves--Alaska--Arctic National Wildlife Refuge. 6. Natural gas--Prospecting--Environmental aspects--Alaska--Arctic National Wildlife Refuge. 7. Arctic National Wildlife Refuge (Alaska) I. Thompson, Tamara, editor of compilation.
    TN872.A7S545 2013
    333.8'23115097987--dc23
                                                            2012042118

Printed in the United States of America
1 2 3 4 5 6 7 17 16 15 14 13

Contents

Introduction

When the US House of Representatives passed a bill to open the Arctic National Wildlife Refuge (ANWR) to oil drilling in February 2012, it wasn't the first time. It was the twelfth time. But like all the previous House attempts to permit oil exploration in the Refuge, that effort was killed by the Senate, casting the longstanding question of drilling in ANWR back to where it has been for more than thirty-five years—in legal limbo.

The history of ANWR and its intended purpose as federally owned land is as conflicted as its potential future. In 1960, President Dwight D. Eisenhower set aside 8.9 million acres in the northeastern corner of Alaska as a wildlife refuge and gave it the legal designation of "wilderness" to forever protect it from development. Twenty years later, Congress expanded the refuge to nineteen million acres but didn't formally designate all of the land as wilderness. Although still a part of the Refuge, 1.5 million acres of the ANWR Coastal Plain (known as Area 1002) were left without the protection of the formal wilderness designation, and Congress authorized studies of the area's natural resources. Congress said that potential oil reserves there should be evaluated but that drilling could proceed only if Congress specifically authorized it. Thus began the thirty-five-year-long political battle over oil exploration at ANWR that continues to the present day.

Although over the years there have been a few legislators in both the Democratic and Republican parties who broke rank when it came time to vote on ANWR legislation, the issue of whether to tap the oil reserve at ANWR has evolved into a sharply divisive political wedge issue. Democrats have fought to keep ANWR off limits for drilling (President Bill Clinton vetoed a 1995 Senate bill that would have allowed drilling, the closest Congress has come to passing such legislation), and Republicans have pressed hard for its development, introducing ANWR bills in each session of Congress, and even including ANWR drilling as part of a federal budget measure. But while Republican efforts to open ANWR have consistently failed, so too have Democrats' efforts to protect the ANWR Coastal Plain by extending the wilderness designation to include Area 1002. The two sides are at an impasse on the issue, and neither one will budge on its position.

The stark political divide on ANWR can be explained most simply in terms of Republican arguments for creating jobs, boosting the economy, and fostering independence from foreign oil versus Democratic arguments for environmental protection, wildlife conservation, and the need to develop alternative energy sources for the longterm. *At Issue* here is the amount of oil in ANWR as it relates to the global oil supply and America's energy future and the potential harm drilling might have on the region's wildlife and sensitive tundra ecosystem, especially the calving grounds of the migratory Porcupine caribou, which lie in Area 1002.

Although nobody knows for sure how much oil is hidden underground in Area 1002, the indicators are favorable; in 1985 the US Geological Survey (USGS) estimated that the Coastal Plain could contain between 5.7 billion to 16 billion barrels of extractable oil. The USGS revised that estimate upward in 2005, saying that new extraction technologies could significantly increase the amount. The Energy Information Administration (EIA) estimates that ANWR drilling would boost US crude production 14 percent and reduce America's need for imported oil by 2 percent. At its peak, ANWR would produce about 0.8 million barrels per day, but America would still need to import about 10.6 million barrels of oil per day to meet its current demands. According to EIA figures, the total amount of oil produced at ANWR would satisfy the country's energy needs for only about nine months.

Drilling opponents see that as a short-sighted solution to an energy problem that will still be around long after ANWR oil runs out. They believe that oil from ANWR would be just a drop in the proverbial bucket to satisfy America's massive appetite for oil, and they say that sacrificing an irreplaceable natural ecosystem to generate such a small short-term result is simply not worth it.

That's the position of President Barack Obama, who has opposed ANWR drilling for many years. In 2007, he told the League of Conservation Voters, "I strongly reject drilling in the Arctic National Wildlife Refuge because it would irreversibly damage a protected national wildlife refuge without creating sufficient oil supplies to meaningfully affect the global market price or have a discernable impact on US energy security."

Drilling opponents say that energy conservation and raising fuel efficiency standards would save far more oil than drilling in ANWR could ever produce, and that the real path to lower prices and American energy security is investing in alternative fuel sources and sustainable clean energy technologies, which would help the country reduce its dependence on foreign oil for generations to come, not just for a few months.

"We can't just drill our way out of the problem," Obama said during an energy policy speech in Indiana on May 6, 2011. "If we're serious about addressing our energy problems, we're going to have to do more than drill."

But with the American economy in a continuing crisis hallmarked by high unemployment and national average gas prices hovering around $4 per gallon, longterm sustainable energy solutions and protecting a remote piece of land most people will never visit don't have the appeal of the more immediate benefits that "drill here, drill now" proponents are touting.

The Congressional Budget Office (CBO) estimates that drilling in ANWR would create more than 735,000 American jobs and generate some $150 billion to $296 billion in leasing and royalties for the federal treasury over the life of production. Additional economic benefits would include stimulating the construction, transportation, and manufacturing sectors nationwide as the operation increases the demand for specific goods and services.

The economic benefits of drilling in ANWR could make the American public—and the lawmakers who represent them—a lot more sympathetic to the idea, something that Republican presidential hopeful Mitt Romney is counting on. In a March 2012 open letter to Alaskan voters, Romney vowed that, "As president, I would push to open new opportunities for America's energy security, onshore and offshore, especially in the Arctic National Wildlife Refuge.... The federal government should be an ally in the effort to develop more of our nation's resources, not an obstacle."

Quite simply, the future of ANWR may depend on which political party wins the White House in 2012 and which has the most seats in Congress following the election. Only time will tell how the politics will play out and whether the ANWR Coastal Plain will be eventually opened for oil development or whether it will be granted the permanent protection of wilderness status. The authors in *At Issue: Should Drilling Be Allowed in the Arctic National Wildlife Refuge?* represent a wide range of viewpoints concerning the oil reserves in ANWR, as well as the potential consequences of its extraction.

1

ANWR Holds America's Greatest Oil Potential

Paul Driessen

Paul Driessen is senior policy advisor for the conservative organizations Congress of Racial Equality and the Committee for a Constructive Tomorrow. He is the author of the book Eco-Imperialism: Green Power—Black Death, *and he writes a column for Townhall.com, a website and print magazine dedicated to conservative politics.*

American anti-drilling policies are one of the main reasons that oil and gas prices are so high. Because there is environmental opposition and political reluctance, American oil resources are effectively locked up, and instead of producing its own oil, the country relies on imported oil. The Arctic National Wildlife Refuge (ANWR) is estimated to hold some 15.6 billion barrels of oil, enough to ease America's energy crunch. Drilling for oil in ANWR would create American jobs, boost tax revenues, increase the domestic energy supply, and lower energy prices a lot faster than alternative energy sources would. ANWR represents America's greatest potential for domestic oil production, and special interest groups have no right to block access to it. Drilling in ANWR should begin right away.

"We can't drill our way out of our energy problem."

This oft-repeated mantra may have superficial appeal. However, on closer examination, it reflects an abysmal grasp of energy and economic facts by special interests that have too much influence over US policies. If only their hot air could be converted into usable energy.

Drilling won't generate production overnight. But it will ensure steady new supplies a few years hence.

Moreover, simply announcing that America is finally hunting oil again would send a powerful signal to global energy markets. It would also tame speculators, many of whom bet that continued US drilling restrictions will further exacerbate the global demand-supply imbalance and send prices even higher for "futures" (under which a person pays a specific amount today, with the expectation of selling a commodity on a future date at a higher price).

Pro-drilling policies would likely bring lower prices, as did past announcements that Brazil had found new offshore oil fields, that Iraq would sign contracts to increase oil production, and that hydraulic fracturing had unlocked enormous new US supplies of natural gas. Conversely, news that supplies are tightening—because of sabotage in Nigeria's delta region, for example, or continued bans on leasing American petroleum—will send prices upward.

We really don't know how much petroleum we have. When "experts" discuss US oil and gas resources and reserves, they are basing their estimates on outdated seismic, drilling and other data and technologies. They often cite reserve estimates that were proven wrong years ago, or treat oil reserves as a fixed number, when in reality reserves are constantly changing and usually increase over time.

"Reserves" are the amount of oil or gas that can be produced at a given price, with existing technology, at a particular point in time, based on actual discoveries and well data, where drilling is permitted and has taken place. "Resources" are the total amount of petroleum geologists believe may be in underground formations, based on what they can "see" with seismic data.

Seismic provides a cross-sectional view of subsurface structures and rock formations that may hold oil, and technological improvements over the past decade have dramatically increased what we can "see," in areas where companies are allowed to do seismic work. 3D seismic and now 4D seismic (how rock formations change over time) paint vivid moving pictures of the subsurface and tell exploration geologists there is much more oil down there than previously estimated.

However, only two-thirds of the Gulf of Mexico and small parts of Alaska are open to offshore operations. The rest of America's offshore areas, along with most onshore federal lands, are off limits to seismic work and drilling. That means we have up-to-date information on only a small portion of our potential energy base. If we can't even use seismic to "see" the vast majority of our underground prospects and resources, we cannot possibly estimate what is actually there! The one thing we can say is our current estimates of US oil and gas resources are wrong, and are almost certainly much too low.

Leasing ANWR prospects would get new oil flowing in 5–10 years. . . . That's far faster than benefits would flow from supposed alternatives.

Understanding resources "in place" is just the first step. To estimate reserves accurately, we have to recognize that drilling technology has also evolved rapidly over the past decade. "Directional drilling" now allows companies to drill wells a mile deep and five miles long, and steer drill bits to penetrate multiple oil zones and hit targets the size of basketball courts. This accuracy, coupled with the ability to fracture rock formations and stimulate them to produce far more oil and gas than previously possible, is simply revolutionary.

In short, our ability to find and capture more of the oil in place has increased our reserves dramatically.

The Arctic National Wildlife Refuge

One of the USA's best prospects is Alaska's Arctic National Wildlife Refuge (ANWR), which geologists say likely contains billions of barrels of recoverable oil. If President Bill Clinton hadn't bowed to Wilderness Society demands and vetoed 1995 legislation, we would be producing a million barrels a day from ANWR right now. That's equal to US imports from Saudi Arabia, at nearly $40 billion annually.

Leasing ANWR prospects would get new oil flowing in 5–10 years, depending in large part on how many lawsuits and other delays prevent drilling. That's far faster than benefits would flow from supposed alternatives: devoting millions more acres of cropland to corn-based (or still non-existent) cellulosic ethanol, persuading millions of people to buy expensive hybrid and flex-fuel cars, building a dozen new nuclear power plants, and blanketing thousands of square miles with wind turbines and solar panels.

These alternatives would take decades to implement, and all face political, legal, technological, economic and environmental hurdles.

Drilling in ANWR and other Alaskan areas would also ensure sufficient production to keep the Trans-Alaska Pipeline (TAP) in operation. Right now, declining North Slope production threatens to reduce oil in the pipeline to the point where it cannot stay sufficiently warm to flow under months-long winter conditions. The TAP needs between 250,000 and 350,000 barrels of oil per day to stay open. If there are inadequate supplies, the pipeline will be abruptly shut down—and even torn down, because current laws require complete removal of the TAP if it stops functioning.

That would result in the sudden elimination of a sizeable portion of our national oil production. It would mean billions of barrels of already discovered oil would be left in the ground and unavailable to American businesses, motorists and other citizens. It would create a huge disincentive to future Arctic oil leasing and development. All of this might please the Sierra Club and Greenpeace, but it is hardly in the national interest.

Drilling and production operations [in ANWR] would impact only 2,000 acres.... Saying this tiny footprint would spoil the refuge is like saying a major airport along South Carolina's northern border would destroy the entire state's scenery and wildlife.

Opening Oil Reserves

ANWR is the size of South Carolina. Its narrow coastal plain is frozen and windswept most of the year. Wildlife flourish amid drilling and production in other Arctic regions, and would do so near ANWR facilities. Inuits who live there know this, and support drilling by an 8:1 margin. Gwich'in Indians who oppose drilling live hundreds of miles away—and have leased and drilled nearly all their own tribal lands, including caribou migratory routes, to generate revenue for the tribe.

Drilling and production operations would impact only 2,000 acres (one-twentieth of Washington, DC), plus narrow roads between drilling sites, to produce some 15 billion gallons of oil annually. Each drill "pad" would support multiple wells that have the capability to reach miles in all directions.

Saying this tiny footprint would spoil the refuge is like saying a major airport along South Carolina's northern border would destroy the entire state's scenery and wildlife. Moreover, the roads would allow caribou and other animals to move around more easily during long, frigid, snowy winters; that would reduce death tolls from starvation and predation, and increase wildlife populations, just as happened elsewhere along the North Slope and TAP route.

Drilling in ANWR is a far better bargain than producing 13 billion gallons of ethanol annually from corn grown on an area nearly as big as Missouri (44 million acres)—using massive amounts of water, pesticides, fertilizer and fossil fuels, and sending corn, food and food aid prices higher and higher. It's far better than using wind to generate enough electricity to power New York City, which would require blanketing Connecticut (3 million acres) with turbines, and putting thousands of eagles, hawks, falcons, whooping cranes and other species at risk of being sliced up by turbine blades.

Proven Reserves

Anti-drilling factions often claim that "US energy prices are high, because Americans consume 25% of the world's oil, while possessing only 3% of its proven oil reserves." The rhetoric is clever, but misleading, even disingenuous, and ultimately harmful.

If unconventional oil and gas reserves are included, the United States will remain a dominant player in world energy markets.

Possession has nothing to do with prices, any more than owning a library, but never opening the books, improves intellectual abilities; or owning farmland that's never tilled feeds hungry people.

The 3% claim refers to now-outdated information about conventional (traditional) oil resources that drilling has confirmed exist and can be produced with then-current technologies and prices. However, American politicians, regulators and courts have made numerous prospects off limits to leasing and delayed or rejected multiple seismic and drilling applications. In so doing, they have ensured that an estimated 170 billion barrels of oil resources in the Outer Continental Shelf, Rockies, Great Lakes, Southwest, ANWR and other federal lands never become "reserves."

In fact, conventional reserves will decrease, as we deplete existing deposits and don't replace them—or we force the TAP to close down, thereby making billions of barrels of proven oil reserves unavailable.

Despite anti-hydrocarbon policies, the United States is still the world's third largest producer of oil, and its largest producer of natural gas. US oil production is actually increasing today, thanks to production from unconventional deposits, mostly on state and private lands. Moreover, our ability to explore unproven areas onshore and offshore has improved exponentially. If unconventional oil and gas reserves are included, the United States will remain a dominant player in world energy markets.

For example, horizontal drilling and hydraulic fracturing ("fracking") has unlocked billions of barrels of oil and trillions of cubic feet of natural gas that just a few years ago were thought to be inaccessible, and have done so with minimal environmental impacts. The new technology has created tens of thousands of direct oilfield jobs, generated billions in revenues, and slashed the price of natural gas by more than 75 percent. Expanded supplies and lower prices for natural gas have spurred a US manufacturing and petrochemical renaissance, creating thousands of additional jobs and billions in additional revenue, and increasing the likelihood that many vehicles will soon run on natural gas.

Leasing and drilling ... translates into additional billions in income tax revenues that oilfield, refinery, manufacturing and other jobs would generate.

Applying 3D seismic, fracking and other new technologies to ANWR and other Arctic prospects would likely increase their reserves and ultimate yield many times over.

The Geological Survey and Congressional Research Service say it's 95% likely that there are 15.6 billion barrels of oil beneath ANWR. With today's prices and fracking technology, 60% of that is recoverable. At $100 a barrel, that represents $1 trillion that we would not have to send to overseas. It means lower prices and reduced risks of oil spills from tankers carrying foreign crude to America.

Stimulating the Economy

Producing ANWR's oil riches represents another $400 billion in state and federal royalties and corporate income taxes, over the life of the fields, plus billions in lease sale revenues, plus thousands of direct and indirect jobs, in addition to numerous jobs created when all this money is reinvested in the USA.

In fact, after the IRS [Internal Revenue Service], the single largest contribution to the US Treasury is oil company oil and gas royalty payments. Companies that produce from federal onshore and offshore leases pay royalties of up to 18% of wellhead prices, and then pay corporate taxes on profits and sales taxes at the pump.

Leasing and drilling also translates into additional billions in income tax revenues that oilfield, refinery, manufacturing and other jobs would generate, and new opportunities for minority, poor and blue collar families to improve their lives and living standards. It means lower prices for gasoline, heating, cooling, food and other products.

Factor in America's other locked-up energy, and we're talking tens of trillions of dollars that we either keep in the United States, by producing that energy . . . or ship overseas.

This energy belongs to all Americans. It's not the private property of environmental pressure groups, or of politicians who cater to them in exchange for re-election support.

This energy is likewise the common heritage of mankind. Politicians and eco-activists have no right to keep it off limits—and tell the rest of the world: "We have no intention of developing American energy. We don't care if you need oil, if soaring food and energy prices are pummeling poor families, or if drilling in your countries harms your habitats to produce oil for US consumers."

Those attitudes are immoral and intolerable. They show disdain for the world's poor. And they are bad for the global environment.

It's time to drill safely and carefully again here in America—onshore and off, in Alaska and the Lower 48—while also developing economically and environmentally sensible new technologies to improve energy conservation, and provide alternatives to petroleum if Earth's hydrocarbon deposits are depleted a century or more from now.

2

ANWR Oil Potential Is Greatly Exaggerated

Richard A. Fineberg

Richard A. Fineberg is an independent, Alaska-based analyst who has reported on economic and environmental issues associated with Alaska petroleum development for more than three decades. He has served as a senior advisor to the governor of Alaska on oil and gas policy, and as a consultant to various state and federal agencies and nongovernmental organizations.

For several reasons, drilling for oil on the Arctic National Wildlife Refuge (ANWR) Coastal Plain is not the silver-bullet solution to oil independence and lower oil prices claimed by proponents of refuge drilling. This analysis, based on 2011 data, shows that over the next two decades reductions in foreign oil imports will account for twenty-five times more oil than ANWR could produce in that same time. The continuing conservation trend, prompted by high oil costs, will reduce oil demand and price increases much more effectively than ANWR drilling. Even with immediate approval of ANWR drilling, only a small fraction of total refuge production would be available oil by 2030, while overstated long-term production claims of drilling advocates often fail to reflect the inherent uncertainty attached to putative long-term prospects. Additionally, to fully tap the estimated production potential of the Arctic Refuge Coastal Plain region would require discovery and development of numerous oil fields scattered across the two million-acre coastal region, affecting a much larger area than the two thousand-acre limit hypothesized by proposed drilling legislation.

The reality of declining U.S. oil imports has stolen much of the thunder from the beguiling but often exaggerated hopes of future benefits from oil that might lie beneath the Coastal Plain of the remote Arctic National Wildlife Refuge. The findings of this report are based primarily on review and analysis of the U.S. Energy Information Administration (EIA) reports on the current U.S. energy picture and Arctic Refuge Coastal Plain region production potential. . . .

The Current U.S. Oil Picture (January 2012)

U.S. net petroleum imports—the EIA's landmark import measurement—have declined significantly in recent years, from approximately 12.5 million barrels per day (bpd) in 2005 to a level below 9.0 million bpd in the agency's 2011 *Annual Energy Outlook.*

This salutary development marks a clear and important trend reversal. (EIA data indicate that between 1985 and 2005 net petroleum imports increased steadily for two decades between 1985 and 2005, peaking in 2005 at 60.3% of total U.S. liquid fuels requirement. By comparison, EIA data indicate that during the first eleven months of 2011, net imports fell to a current average of 45.4% of the nation's total liquid fuels requirement.)

The upward trajectory of oil prices since 1998 appears to be the principal cause of this significant trend reversal.

High oil prices are apt to induce pro-drilling frenzies, setting the stage for unwise public policy decisions.

The Arctic Refuge Coastal Plain: Geologic Background

Based on a three-year study concluded in 1998, the USGS [US Geological Survey] assessment team determined that "[t]he total quantity of technically recoverable oil within the entire assessment area is estimated to be between 5.7 and 16.0 billion barrels (95-percent and 5-percent probability range), with a mean value of 10.4 billion barrels."

Only a fraction of the 10.4 billion barrels of oil that might be discovered beneath the Arctic Refuge Coastal Plain would be produced between now and 2030.

USGS analysts have noted that their three-year study precluded the possibility of finding that oil in one super-giant field like Prudhoe Bay, the largest field ever discovered in the United States. From study data, it appears that if discovery and oil prices warrant production, oil might be produced from as many as 40-odd fields, which might be discovered in as many as nine different geologic plays (rock structures capable of holding oil).

The EIA Looks Ahead (January 2012)

Over the next two decades EIA anticipates continued reductions to imported crude oil far outweigh the amount of oil that could reasonably be anticipated from oil development on the Arctic Refuge Coastal Plain region.

EIA's basic 2005 energy development scenario anticipated 113.2 billion barrels of net oil imports between 2012 and 2030; the corresponding figure in the agency's 2011 *Annual Energy Outlook* Reference Case scenario was 66.3 billion barrels. These figures represent a 46.9 billion barrel reduction in forecasted petroleum imports over this six-year period.

Due to logistical constraints, the EIA reports only a fraction of the 10.4 billion barrels of oil that might be discovered beneath the Arctic Refuge Coastal Plain would be produced between now and 2030. Based on EIA's 2011 Mean Resource Case scenario, immediate authorization of drilling in the Arctic Refuge Coastal Plain region would have resulted in production of approximately 1.8 billion barrels of crude oil between 2021 and 2030.

The ratio between estimated oil import reductions and oil production from the Arctic Refuge Coastal Plain region between 2012 and 2030 was approximately twenty-five to one (25:1).

The claim that the Arctic Refuge could be developed from a 2,000-acre "postage-stamp" base on the Coastal Plain is misleading.

Assuming a real (inflation-adjusted) future oil price of $100 per barrel, between 2012 and 2030 the U.S. was on track to reduce cash payments for foreign crude oil by $4,685 billion (nearly $4.7 trillion). This figure represents money formerly tied up in petroleum imports that would be free to be spent on other domestic needs.

The assignment of a similar value to the barrels of oil that might be found beneath the Arctic Refuge Coastal Plain region over the same 19-year period would reduce cash payments for imported oil by $180 billion ($0.18 trillion).

To achieve the full potential of production from the Arctic Refuge Coastal Plain region would require the discovery and development of numerous oil fields scattered across the Arctic Refuge Coastal Plain region. For this reason, the claim that the Arctic Refuge could be developed from a 2,000-acre "postage-stamp" base on the Coastal Plain is misleading.

EIA's 2011 data indicate that 35.0 billion barrels of the 2012–2030 import reduction represents reduced consumption of liquid fuels; 11.9 billion barrels was attributable to increased production of domestic liquid fuel supplies, including increased petroleum production and increased alternative sources such as ethanol and biodiesel. . . .

Conservation Through 2030: A Much Better Investment

Production claims tendered by drilling advocates are often unrealistically optimistic because they fail to acknowledge the low probability associated with high forecast estimates.

In addition to the risks inherent in frontier petroleum development, the current and anticipated reductions in imports between 2012 and 2030 delineated in this analysis strongly support the wisdom of continuing on the demonstrably effective path of conservation.

The information generated in this report provides strong empirical support for opposing petroleum exploration and development in the Arctic Refuge Coastal Plain region.

The 25:1 ratio between reduced oil imports anticipated by EIA and oil production from the Arctic Refuge Coastal Plain region between now and 2030 heralds the establishment of a conservation policy that may be the best bet to take this nation safely out of these woods by completing the reversal of the previous, longstanding trend of increasing dependence on foreign crude oil supplies.

When U.S. financial capital is needed for major investment in national priorities that include education, health care, infrastructure renewal and energy alternatives, it is difficult to justify diverting a significant portion of that capital to petroleum development in the Arctic Refuge Coastal Plain region.

3

Drill, Already

National Review

National Review *provides conservative commentary on American politics, news, and culture.*

Drilling for oil in America in areas that are currently off-limits, such as the Arctic National Wildlife Refuge (ANWR), represents the best way for America to achieve energy independence and decrease its reliance on foreign oil sources. Opening just 0.01 percent of ANWR to oil and natural gas development could supply 5 percent of America's oil for twelve years, which would have far-reaching economic benefits. Domestic oil production would also decrease our dependence on foreign oil. There are no good arguments for keeping the oil supply in ANWR off the market.

With the end of Memorial Day weekend comes the beginning of summer, and with it the beginning of America's heaviest driving season as millions of Americans take to the highways for summer breaks. But if recent trends hold, vacationers are likely to put fewer miles on their odometers this summer than last. High gas prices are finally curbing America's demand for the open road. Transportation Department statistics for March indicate that the country just experienced its first year-over-year decline in miles driven since 1979.

A decrease in demand is one natural market response to rising gas prices. The other natural response—an increase in supply—has not been as forthcoming, and the price of oil continues to rise even though Americans are driving less. The

Organization of Petroleum Exporting Countries (OPEC) is partly to blame for this market recalcitrance; the international oil cartel manipulates supply in order keep oil prices high. But if members of Congress really want to mitigate the effects of high oil prices as much as they claim they do, they could start by letting oil companies bring America's vast untapped supplies to market.

With oil nearing $130 a barrel, there are no good arguments left for keeping this supply off the market.

We're not just talking about the Alaskan National Wildlife Reserve (ANWR)—which Congress stupidly keeps off-limits even though proposed oil exploration there would only affect approximately 2,000 of its 19 million acres—though opening just that 0.01 percent of ANWR to oil and natural gas development could supply 5 percent of America's oil per year for 12 years before it starts to decline, according to Energy Department estimates. The Outer Continental Shelf—also off-limits to drilling—likely contains billions of barrels of additional oil and natural gas reserves. While Fidel Castro's Cuba saw no compunction about leasing its share of these waters to the Chinese, the U.S. continues to forbid oil and natural gas exploration in its share.

Critics of proposals to open these areas for business argue that they will take up to 10 years to bring any new supplies online. Of course, they were using this same argument 10 years ago, and if they hadn't prevailed then the U.S. would be less dependent on foreign oil today. They also argue that Congress should be encouraging renewable energy sources such as solar power, wind and biofuels rather than opening the spigots on new sources of petroleum. But the simple fact of the matter is that solar power and wind can't fulfill the vital role non-renewables play in the U.S. economy. As for biofuels, the 2007 mandate requiring the production of 36 billion gallons by 2022 has exacerbated an increase in world food prices without doing anything to lessen the pain at the pump.

Receiving no help from their leaders, Americans have taken it upon themselves to achieve savings in the face of skyrocketing fuel costs. Simply put, we are driving less. Now it's time for Congress to meet us halfway. Superior U.S. technology has made it possible to drill in the environmentally sensitive areas off our coasts with minimal disturbance to the surrounding ecosystem. Better increased production in the U.S. than in other countries with worse environmental track records. With oil nearing $130 a barrel, there are no good arguments left for keeping this supply off the market. If members of Congress really care about helping Americans who are sacrificing in the wake of high gas prices, the best thing they can do is just get out of the way.

4

ANWR Drilling Will Not Reduce America's Dependence on Foreign Oil

Natural Resources Defense Council

The Natural Resources Defense Council (NRDC) is a nonprofit membership organization that advocates for the preservation of the environment worldwide. The NRDC has strongly and consistently opposed opening the Arctic National Wildlife Refuge to oil exploration and production.

Despite the fact that both Congress and the American people have been overwhelmingly clear and consistent that they want the Arctic National Wildlife Refuge (AMWR) permanently protected rather than opened for oil exploration, "Big Oil" is pushing harder than ever to gain access to what it believes would be a hugely profitable and game-changing venture. Producing domestic oil for energy independence is not the real issue here; the real issue is profits and lifting barriers to the private development of mineral resources on public and protected lands nationwide, which would be a huge boon to the oil industry. In and of itself, ANWR oil is nothing more than a drop in the proverbial bucket, and it would do very little to further American energy independence. As one of the world's most extensive and pristine wilderness areas, ANWR should not be sacrificed for the false illusion of energy security.

On the northern edge of our continent, stretching from the peaks of the Brooks Range across a vast expanse of tundra to the Beaufort Sea, lies Alaska's Arctic National Wildlife Refuge. An American Serengeti, the Arctic Refuge continues to pulse with million-year-old ecological rhythms. It is the greatest living reminder that conserving nature in its wild state is a core American value.

In affirmation of that value, Congress and the American people have consistently made clear their desire to protect this treasure and rejected claims that drilling for oil in the Arctic Refuge is any sort of answer to the nation's dependence on foreign oil. Twice in 2005, Congress acted explicitly to defend the refuge from the (President George W.) Bush administration and pro-drilling forces, with House leaders removing provisions that would have allowed for drilling from a massive budget bill, and the Senate withstanding an attempt by Republican leaders to open up the Arctic.

Since then, concerned Americans have continued to push Congress to thwart recurring efforts to see the refuge spoiled. During President (Barack) Obama's 2008 campaign he pledged not to open the coastal plain of the Arctic National Wildlife Refuge to oil and gas leasing. Over the last year (2011) the Fish and Wildlife Service has been developing a new management plan for the Refuge and is considering recommending Wilderness for the coastal plain.

Opening the Arctic Refuge to energy development is about transferring our public estate into corporate hands so it can be liquidated for a quick buck.

Americans Oppose Drilling the Arctic National Wildlife Refuge

The controversy over drilling in the Arctic Refuge—the last piece of America's Arctic coastline not already open to oil exploration—isn't new. Big Oil has long sought access to the refuge's coastal plain, a fragile swath of tundra that teems with staggering numbers of birds and animals. During the Bush administration's first term, repeated attempts were made to open the refuge. But time after time, the American public rejected the idea.

Congress has received hundreds of thousands of emails, faxes and phone calls from citizens opposed to drilling in the Arctic Refuge, an outpouring that has helped make the difference. And polls have consistently shown that a majority of Americans oppose drilling, even in the face of high gas prices and misleading claims from oil interests. A June 2008 poll by the research firm Belden Russonello & Stewart found that 55 percent of the American public supports continued protection for the Arctic Refuge, and only 35 percent of Americans believe that allowing oil companies to drill in the refuge would result in lower gas prices for American consumers.

Despite repeated failure and stiff opposition, drilling proponents press on. Why? They believe that opening the Arctic Refuge will turn the corner in the broader national debate over whether or not energy, timber, mining and other industries should be allowed into pristine wild areas across the country. Along with the Arctic, oil interests are now targeting America's protected coastal waters. Next up: Greater Yellowstone? Our Western canyonlands?

The drive to drill in the Arctic Refuge is about oil company profits and lifting barriers to future exploration in protected lands, pure and simple. It has nothing to do with energy independence. Opening the Arctic Refuge to energy development is about transferring our public estate into corporate hands so that it can be liquidated for a quick buck.

Arctic Refuge Oil Is a Distraction, Not a Solution

What would America gain by allowing heavy industry into the refuge? Very little. Oil from the refuge would hardly make a dent in our dependence on foreign imports—leaving our economy and way of life just as exposed to wild swings in worldwide oil prices and supply as it is today. The truth is, we simply can't drill our way to energy independence.

It would take 10 years for any Arctic Refuge oil to reach the market, and even when production peaks—in the distant year of 2027—the refuge would produce a paltry 3 percent of Americans' daily consumption. The U.S. government's own Energy Information Agency recently reported that drilling in the Arctic would save less than 4 cents per gallon in 20 years. Whatever oil the refuge might produce is simply irrelevant to the larger issue of meeting America's future energy needs.

The solution to America's energy problems will be found in American ingenuity, not more oil.

Oil produced from the Arctic Refuge would come at an enormous, and irreversible, cost. The refuge is among the world's last true wildernesses, and it is one of the largest sanctuaries for Arctic animals. Traversed by a dozen rivers and framed by jagged peaks, this spectacular wilderness is a vital birthing ground for polar bears, grizzlies, Arctic wolves, caribou and the endangered shaggy musk ox, a mammoth-like survivor of the last Ice Age.

For a sense of what Big Oil's heavy machinery would do to the refuge, just look 60 miles west to Prudhoe Bay—a gargantuan oil complex that has turned 1,000 square miles of fragile tundra into a sprawling industrial zone containing 1,500 miles of roads and pipelines, 1,400 producing wells and three jetports. The result is a landscape defaced by mountains of sewage sludge, scrap metal, garbage and more than 60 contaminated waste sites that contain—and often leak—acids, lead, pesticides, solvents and diesel fuel.

While proponents of drilling insist that the Arctic Refuge could be developed by disturbing as little as 2,000 acres with the 1.5-million-acre coastal plain, an NRDC [N sources Defense Council] analysis reveals this to be pure myth. Why? Because U.S. Geological Survey studies have found that oil in the refuge isn't concentrated in a single, large reservoir. Rather, it's spread across the coastal plain in more than 30 small deposits, which would require vast networks of roads and pipelines that would fragment the habitat, disturbing and displacing wildlife.

A Responsible Path to Energy Security

The solution to America's energy problems will be found in American ingenuity, not more oil. Only by reducing our reliance on oil—foreign and domestic—and investing in cleaner, renewable forms of power will our country achieve true energy security.

The good news is that we already have many of the tools we need to accomplish this. For example, Detroit [Michigan] has the technology right now to produce high-performance hybrid cars, trucks and SUVs. If America made the transition to these more efficient vehicles, far more oil would be saved than the Arctic Refuge is likely to produce. Doesn't that make far more sense than selling out our natural heritage and exploiting one of our true wilderness gems?

5

ANWR Should Be Permanently Protected from Drilling

Paul Alaback et al.

To mark the fiftieth anniversary of the Arctic National Wildlife Refuge, more than one hundred and sixty leading scientists and natural resource managers in the United States and Canada signed this letter to US President Barack Obama, urging him to permanently protect the Refuge from oil exploration and drilling.

In 1980, Congress enlarged the wilderness area first set aside by President Dwight D. Eisenhower, renaming it the Arctic National Wildlife Refuge (ANWR) and broadening its mission to include international research and management and traditional uses by the area's indigenous people. Only the coastal plain area was omitted, and this is a glaring oversight because it is an ecologically important area that supports incredible wildlife diversity. It also serves as the calving ground for the migratory Porcupine caribou herd, on whose health the local indigenous people depend. Because it is heretofore untouched and its elements of ecology so deeply intertwined, this pristine area is an important resource for researchers. Any disturbance or development on the coastal plain would have far-ranging effects on the stability and health of the region's whole ecosystem. The health of the coastal plain is integral to the health of ANWR as a whole, and it is urgent that the coastal plain area be given permanent protection as wilderness.

D ear Mr. President:

As scientists and natural resource managers from the United States and Canada with many years of experience in ecology, wildlife and conservation biology, resource management, and cultural anthropology, we encourage your administration to permanently secure the ecological integrity of the coastal plain of the Arctic National Wildlife Refuge.

The wildlands of the Arctic Refuge include the barrier islands and estuaries of the Beaufort Sea, the Arctic coastal plain, the Brooks Range, and the boreal forest within the upper Yukon River watershed. First set aside by President Dwight D. Eisenhower as the Arctic National Wildlife Range in 1960, this is the only conservation unit in the United States that encompasses an intact Arctic ecosystem. Combined with the adjacent Ivvavik and Vuntut national parks in Canada, the Arctic Refuge represents one of the largest protected landscapes in the world. Moreover, the Arctic Refuge's coastal plain is a rare example of an ecosystem where ecological and cultural processes continue to interact much as they have for thousands of years. Unlike the adjoining refuge lands that are designated Wilderness, the coastal plain is not permanently protected from development.

The Mission of the Refuge

When President Eisenhower established the Arctic National Wildlife Range, he had the foresight and wisdom to include the entire ecosystem both south and north of the Brooks Range, encompassing the biologically rich coastal plain considered essential to the integrity of this ecosystem. In 1980, Congress enlarged the range to encompass additional wildlife habitat and designated this unique area the Arctic National Wildlife Refuge [ANWR]. The refuge mission was broadened to include international research and management, as well as support for subsistence uses that form the basis of Native cultural values. Most of the original wildlife range was designated as Wilderness. Only the 1.5-million-acre coastal plain was omitted. And today, this oversight remains a significant conservation concern.

Oil and gas exploration and development [in ANWR] would have a major effect on water resources.

Olaus Murie, who initiated the first biological studies of Alaska's caribou herds and was instrumental in the establishment of the Refuge, stressed the value of the area for long-term study and research of Arctic ecosystems. Six decades of biological study and scientific research have confirmed that the coastal plain of the Arctic National Wildlife Refuge forms a vital component of the biological diversity of the refuge and merits the same kind of permanent safeguards and precautionary management as the rest of this original conservation unit. In contrast to the broad (greater than 150 mi.) coastal plain to the west of the Arctic Refuge, the coastal plain within the refuge is much narrower (15–40 mi.). This unique compression of habitats concentrates the occurrence of a wide variety of species, including polar bears, grizzly bears, wolves, wolverines, caribou, muskoxen, Dolly Varden, Arctic Grayling, snow geese, and more than 130 species of migratory birds. In fact, according to the U.S. Fish & Wildlife Service, the Arctic Refuge coastal plain contains the greatest wildlife diversity of any protected area above the Arctic Circle.

Caribou Calving Grounds

The coastal plain provides essential calving and post-calving habitat for the Porcupine Caribou Herd, the largest (at about 100,000 animals) international migratory caribou herd in the world. The United States and Canada share the immense responsibility of managing this herd and protecting the key habitats on which the herd depends. In 1987, the two nations signed an international agreement to protect the Porcupine Caribou Herd. Since then, the calving grounds on the Canadian side of the border have received full protection, while the United States has not yet taken similar steps to adequately protect this important habitat within the coastal plain of the Arctic Refuge—the historic and traditional calving grounds of the Porcupine Caribou Herd. The Gwich'in Nation of Alaska and Canada depends upon the sustained productivity of the Porcupine Caribou Herd and are justifiably concerned about its security. Extensive state and university research on the Central Arctic Caribou Herd at Prudhoe Bay indicates appreciable losses of preferred calving habitats in response to petroleum development and associated decline in reproductive success for those animals displaced by development. These findings were supported by the National Research Council's 2003 report *Cumulative Environmental Effects of North Slope Oil and Gas Activities on Alaska's North Slope.*

Biologists have also identified conservation concerns with other wildlife populations in the Arctic Refuge, including threatened polar bears, muskoxen, and snow geese. Although many polar bears den on the pack ice, bears are increasingly denning on shore and the refuge's coastal plain is the most important land denning area for Beaufort Sea bears in Alaska. Muskoxen are year-round residents of the coastal plain, and disturbance from industrial development, particularly in winter, holds the potential to increase energetic costs and result in decreased calf production. Also, snow geese might be displaced from important feeding and staging habitats prior to autumn migration, increasing energy expenditure and reducing their ability to accumulate the fat needed for migration. The coastal plain serves many biological functions, including nesting habitat for shorebirds, waterfowl, songbirds, raptors, and other migratory birds.

Disruptive Ecological Changes

The Interior Department predicts that oil and gas exploration and development would have a major effect on water resources. Fresh water already is limited on the refuge's coastal plain, and direct damage to wetlands will adversely affect fish, waterfowl, and other migratory birds. These potentially disruptive effects to fish and wildlife should not be viewed in isolation, however.

> *The 110-mile-long coastal plain of the Arctic National Wildlife Refuge encompasses 1.5 million acres of key wildlife habitat vital to the integrity of the Arctic National Wildlife Refuge.*

Arctic ecosystems are characterized by many complex interactions, and changes to one component may have secondary but significant effects on other ecosystem components. Oil exploration and development have substantially changed environments where they have occurred in Alaska's central Arctic. Since the discovery of oil at Prudhoe Bay in 1968, the National Research Council estimated in 2003 that development affects a land area of about 1,000 square miles of Arctic habitats, which represented one of the world's largest industrial complexes. Oil spills, contaminated waste, and other sources of pollution have had measurable impacts on this environment. Roads, pipelines, well pads, processing facilities, and other support infrastructure have incrementally altered the character of this ecosystem.

ANWR Is a Climate Change Resource

Pronounced ecological changes in the flora and fauna at the landscape level have been observed in the Alaskan Arctic in recent decades as a consequence of climate change. The Arctic Refuge, with no direct ecosystem effects as yet from development, is serving an essential role in the joint efforts by state, federal, and regional natural resource agencies, academia, and environmental NGOs [nongovernmental organizations] that are monitoring ecological changes in the Alaskan Arctic. This investigative work must continue to provide the baseline information necessary to guide future oil, gas, and other resource exploration and development activities in the Alaskan Arctic. In addition, should habitat distribution shift as a result of climate change, wildlife will have a better opportunity to adapt in an unfragmented ecosystem. The refuge and adjacent areas in Canada are especially important given that many other areas of the Beaufort Sea Coastal Plain are already impacted by resource development—or will be under future development. Based on our current collective experience and understanding of the cumulative effects of oil and gas exploration and development on Alaska's North Slope, we do not believe the impacts from development activities, as well as those effects resulting from the changing climate, have been adequately considered for the Arctic Refuge. Mitigation efforts associated with oil and gas development without adequate data on this complex ecosystem and changing climate are unlikely to prove successful.

Please understand that we are not philosophically opposed to oil and gas development in Alaska. Indeed, we all clearly recognize the need for balanced resource management. But we also recognize the importance of maintaining the biological diversity and ecosystem integrity of our nation's Arctic. Nearly the entire Arctic Coast of Alaska north of the Brooks Range is available for oil and gas exploration or development. The 110-mile-long coastal plain of the Arctic National Wildlife Refuge encompasses 1.5 million acres of key wildlife habitat vital to the integrity of the Arctic National Wildlife Refuge.

An Historic Opportunity for Preservation

As we celebrate the 50th anniversary of the Arctic National Wildlife Refuge, we encourage you to take this historic opportunity to safeguard the extraordinary natural values of the coastal plain. We are concerned that persistent efforts to mandate oil development will be successful unless administrative or legislative action provides permanent protection for this national conservation unit. Your administration has the opportunity to help safeguard the ecological integrity of this important national conservation system unit for future generations of Americans.

We urge you, Mr. President, to implement administrative actions and support legislation, as appropriate, that may be needed to permanently protect, for future generations, the biological diversity and wilderness character of the coastal plain of the Arctic National Wildlife Refuge.

6

ANWR Oil Production Delay Is Unnecessary

Jon Basil Utley

Jon Basil Utley is associate publisher of The American Conservative *and a former foreign correspondent for Knight Ridder newspapers. He has decades of experience in the oil business, including as the owner and operator of a small oil drilling partnership.*

Environmentalists claim that pursuing alternative power sources is the best solution for America's energy woes because it would take the Arctic National Wildlife Refuge (ANWR) a decade or more to produce oil. But the reason for the delay is political, not geographic or technical. It is because there are so many barriers to American energy development, namely environmental regulations and cumbersome and antiquated leasing procedures. Environmental lawsuits notoriously grind the development process to a halt, thus delaying the beginning of well productivity. Drilling in ANWR could generate massive amounts of new oil very quickly if it is simply allowed to happen. Laws need to be changed in order to speed the process. Other countries can get new energy sources online fairly quickly, and there should be no reason the United States can't do the same by fast-tracking the opening of ANWR for oil development.

The media constantly repeat the claim that it would take a decade to get the Arctic National Wildlife Refuge (ANWR) into oil production and about as long for offshore continental oil to start flowing. Most accounts promote the views of extreme environmentalists to make the issue appear so hopeless that we must instead "change our way of life" rather than tap into proven oil reserves. In July (2008), CNN repeatedly reported that offshore drilling would take "seven to 10 years" to get into production. Yet Brazil's Petrobras expects its new finds in extraordinarily deep waters to already be producing 100,000 barrels per day in just two years. What is wrong with American oil companies that they would take so long?

In fact, the world oil shortage is political, not geological. In the U.S., the government makes it virtually impossible to drill in new areas offshore. In Nigeria, civil strife has shut down major production. In Libya and Iran, Washington effectively blockaded and isolated the nations for years to inhibit new production. In Iraq, of course, the U.S. destroyed much of the infrastructure since the first Gulf war in 1991 and then blockaded reconstruction. In nations such as Russia and Mexico nationalism and corruption curtail increased production.

At full production, ANWR would add a million barrels per day to U.S. production.

U.S. Needs a More Effective System

Outside of developed Western countries, the single largest reason for oil "shortages" is government incompetence and ownership of the subsoil rights so that landowners don't benefit from oil discoveries. In Patagonia, Argentina (a nation with abundant oil), I was told how it was common for landowners to try to hide any evidence of oil seepages from underground, lest the government oil company come in and ruin their lands with no benefit to themselves. Private mineral rights ownership is the reason some 90 percent of all oil wells drilled have been in the U.S. Scientific advances and innovative engineers keep coming up with ways to both discover new fields and keep old ones in production almost indefinitely.

ANWR could become the fastest way to generate hundreds of billions of dollars of new oil. But laws need to be changed to fast track the leasing (there are 11 litigation choke points) and to create special courts to expedite environmental issues, as recently proposed by Rep. Michele Bachman (R-Minn.). Under current laws, it could indeed take 10 years to produce oil, compared to two or three years for the actual drilling and pumping. Additionally, leasing is done slowly, thanks to laws written when oil was plentiful. Such laws were designed to gain maximum upfront money for the government, not for speed. For example, BP recently paid $1.2 billion for a new offshore lease, some 400 miles east of Alaska's Prudhoe Bay. The cost and distance gives some idea of industry expectations as to the extent of oil reserves.

Drilling . . . will not spoil the richness and abundance of Alaska's wildlife.

Environmental Slowdowns

In Anchorage last month [July 2008], Marilyn Crockett, executive director of the Alaska Oil & Gas Association, explained to me the following time frame for ANWR drilling: Expect 12 months or more for an Environmental Impact Statement after Congress approves drilling. And this is working fast. It would likely take much longer. Expect 12 months to 18 months for the Department of Interior to draw up and bid out the lease-sale process. Plan on two years for oil companies to do test drilling and analysis. Drilling and transport of heavy equipment can only be done in the winter months when the permafrost ground is solidly frozen, from December through April. Concurrently with oil drilling, a 75-mile pipeline spur needs be built to connect to the main Alyeska Pipeline from Prudhoe Bay to the Southern shipping port.

However, this time frame does not allow for environmental lawsuits "every step of the way," as Crockett warned. The rest of the 10-year time frame is to allow for lawsuits trying to prevent or harass production in one way or another. For example, a single judge in California's 9th circuit has failed to issue a decision on a Shell Oil project that already had $200 million of investment before it was ordered to stop. It will produce 30,000 barrels per day, about $1 billion per year of oil.

Big Payoff for a Small Footprint

There has already been a test well drilled in ANWR and the oil drilling could be done from a concentrated small area, about the size of Dulles Airport [in Virginia]. Compare this to the total size of ANWR, which is roughly equivalent to the size of South Carolina. Its reserves are estimated at 10 billion barrels by the U.S. Geological Survey, compared to 32 billion nationwide, almost a 33 percent increase. At full production, ANWR would add a million barrels per day to U.S. production. At $100 per barrel, this would equal over $36 billion per year that would not need to be spent on foreign oil. It would also create some 700,000 well-paying jobs, according to a Wharton Econometrics study.

Some accurate pictures are finally beginning to circulate. Previously, ANWR was typically portrayed as if it was like the Rockies, with happy goats jumping around. But the land is actually flat and desolate for most of the year, feeding birds and caribou in the summertime. I have personally seen such land with its untold numbers of shallow, frigid little lakes on the Arctic Circle in Northern Russia. It reminded me of what the first French explorer called such lands in Canada's northern extremes: "The Land God Gave to Cain." I was in Alaska hiking last July [2008]; the quantity and variety of animal life is astounding. Grizzly bears roam within the city limits of Anchorage and moose die of starvation every winter all over the state. Nearly a million caribou (reindeer) roam. The whole western half of the state is without roads. Hundreds of streams are filled with salmon. I saw a bowhead whale breaching and little sea otters (once nearly extinct) in Seward Harbour during one afternoon boat trip out into the bay. Drilling, in other words, will not spoil the richness and abundance of Alaska's wildlife.

Interesting Facts About Alaskan Oil

- Drilling is permitted in the Beaufort Sea on Alaska's north coast. On the west coast, it is not allowed under the general prohibition against offshore drilling.

- New technology now also allows long distance slant and horizontal drilling from a single drill site. BP is now planning such an eight-mile drill.

- The Beaufort Sea off shore is very shallow and production is done from man-made islands. A single platform allows for many slant wells.

- The Bering Sea between Alaska and Siberia is only some 200 feet to 300 feet deep.

- Estimates of recoverable oil are based on a $40 barrel price—they should be much higher with oil at $100-plus per barrel. The higher price justifies more costly drilling and secondary recovery engineering.

- Alyeska Pipeline once pumped 2.1 million barrels of oil per day, It's now at 700,000 and declining 7 percent annually. Roughly 400,000 of these barrels come from many new, smaller fields discovered after Prudhoe Bay started production.

- The Alaska National Petroleum Reserve, a very large area west of Prudhoe Bay, may also have large new oil reserves. However, most of the area has not yet been leased by the Federal government's very slow plan, nor explored, nor litigated.

Washington needs to declare a national emergency program to produce energy. The reasons we don't are political, not technical.

The amounts of natural gas are just as astounding as the quantities of oil. The U.S. Geological Survey estimated years ago that there were 150 trillion cubic feet of conventional gas, 590 trillion cubic feet of gas hydrates (an as-yet-unexploited form of methane trapped in water molecules underground). The U.S. Geological Survey estimated that to be "twice the amount of carbon to be found in all known fossil fuels on Earth." Also, there is an uncalculated amount of drillable coal-bed methane in an estimated 13.7 billion tons of indicated coal resources.

The state government of Alaska is now proposing a new pipeline to transport already discovered gas through Canada to connect with pipelines reaching the American Midwest and the east. It will cost around $30 billion, be underground, and transport quantities equal to some 6 percent to 8 percent of all current U.S. consumption.

The Need for Political Solutions

Meanwhile, Washington has become paralyzed by dysfunctional government. France and China can build nuclear electric plants in just years; in the U.S. it takes a decade. Brazil will bring offshore oil online in 24 months, while for U.S. companies it takes 10 years. New refineries are virtually illegal to build. New electricity-generating plants using coal are now unable to obtain financing because of environment constraints.

This is destroying the value of the dollar and wrecking our balance of trade, making oil prohibitively expensive, and sending hundreds of billions of dollars to foreign lands—many of whom are no friends of America. No wonder 80 percent of Americans think their nation is on the wrong track. Washington needs to declare a national emergency program to produce energy. The reasons we don't are political, not technical.

7

ANWR Drilling Could Further Compromise Shrinking Caribou Herd

Charles J. Hanley

Pulitzer Prize-winning journalist Charles J. Hanley is a special correspondent for the Associated Press wire service.

The Porcupine caribou herd, which migrates through the Arctic National Wildlife Refuge (ANWR) to and from its calving gounds there, has dwindled from more than 178,000 animals in 1989 to just around 100,000 today. The indigenous Gwich'in people—the "People of the Caribou"—rely on the herd for their physical, spiritual, and cultural survival. Protecting the health and safety of the Porcupine caribou herd—and thereby protecting the health and safety of the Gwich'in—has been one of the major reasons environmentalists oppose oil development in ANWR. Recent pressures from global warming have worked to thin the Porcupine herd and others like it, and there is no sign of recovery. Any additional stresses on the animals, such as may be caused by oil exploration or drilling, could further compromise the weakened herd and put the traditional Gwich'in way of life in jeopardy.

Here on the endlessly rolling and tussocky terrain of northwest Canada, where man has hunted caribou since the Stone Age, the vast antlered herds are fast growing thin. And it's not just here.

Across the tundra 1,000 miles to the east, Canada's Beverly herd, numbering more than 200,000 a decade ago, can barely be found today.

Halfway around the world in Siberia, the biggest aggregation of these migratory animals, of the dun-colored herds whose sweep across the Arctic's white canvas is one of nature's matchless wonders, has shrunk by hundreds of thousands in a few years.

From wildlife spectacle to wildlife mystery, the decline of the caribou—called reindeer in the Eurasian Arctic—has biologists searching for clues, and finding them.

They believe the insidious impact of climate change, its tipping of natural balances and disruption of feeding habits, is decimating a species that has long numbered in the millions and supported human life in Earth's most inhuman climate.

Many herds have lost more than half their number from the maximums of recent decades, a global survey finds. They "hover on the precipice of a major decline," it says.

The Porcupine herd moves over a 100,000-square-mile range, calving in the Arctic National Wildlife Refuge.

Sensing Trouble

The "People of the Caribou," the Native Gwich'in of the Yukon and Alaska, were among the first to sense trouble, in the late 1990s, as their Porcupine herd dwindled. From 178,000 in 1989, the herd—named for the river crossing its range—is now estimated to number 100,000.

"They used to come through by the hundreds," James Firth, 56, of the Gwich'in Renewable Resources Board said as he guided two Associated Press journalists across the tundra.

Off toward distant horizons this summer afternoon, only small groups of a dozen or fewer migrating caribou could be seen grazing southward across the spongy landscape, green with a layer of grasses, mosses and lichen over the Arctic permafrost.

"I've never seen it like this before," Firth said of the sparse numbers.

More than 50 identifiable caribou herds migrate over huge wilderness tracts in a wide band circling the top of the world. They head north in the spring to ancient calving grounds, then back south through summer and fall to winter ranges closer to northern forests.

The Porcupine herd moves over a 100,000-square-mile range, calving in the Arctic National Wildlife Refuge of northeast Alaska, where proposals for oil drilling have long stirred opposition from environmentalists seeking to protect the caribou.

Global Warming Effects

The global survey by researchers at the University of Alberta, published in June [2009] in the peer-reviewed journal *Global Change Biology*, has deepened concerns about the caribou's future.

Global warming has boosted temperatures in the Arctic twice as much as elsewhere, and Canadian researchers say the natural balance is suffering.

Drawing on scores of other studies, government databases, wildlife management boards and other sources, the biologists found that 34 of 43 herds being monitored worldwide are in decline. The average falloff in numbers was 57 percent from earlier maximums, they said.

Siberia's Taimyr herd has declined from 1 million in 2000 to an estimated 750,000, as reported in the 2008 "Arctic Report Card" of the U.S. National Oceanic and Atmospheric Administration.

The Taimyr is the world's largest herd, but Canada and Alaska have more caribou, and the Alberta study reported that 22 of 34 North American herds are shrinking. Data were insufficient to make a judgment on seven others.

In an interview, Liv Solveig Vors, the June report's lead author, summarized what is believed behind the caribou crash: "Climate change is changing the way they're interacting with their food, directly and indirectly."

Global warming has boosted temperatures in the Arctic twice as much as elsewhere, and Canadian researchers say the natural balance is suffering:

- Unusual freezing rains in autumn are locking lichen, the caribou's winter forage, under impenetrable ice sheets. This was the documented cause in the late 1990s of the near-extinction of the 50,000-strong Peary caribou subspecies on Canada's High Arctic islands.

- Mosquitoes, flies and insect parasites have always tormented and weakened caribou, but warmer temperatures have aggravated this summertime problem, driving the animals on crazed, debilitating runs to escape, and keeping them from foraging and fattening up for winter.

- The springtime Arctic "green-up" is occurring two weeks or more earlier. The great caribou migrations evolved over ages to catch the shrubs on the calving grounds at their freshest and most nutritious. But pregnant, migrating cows may now be arriving too late.

Vors said caribou are unlikely to adjust.

"Evolutionary changes tend to take place over longer time scales than the time scale of climate change at the moment," she said. Climatologists foresee northern temperatures rising several degrees more this century unless global greenhouse gas emissions are sharply reduced soon.

Radical Declines

Caribou herds have gone through boom-and-bust cycles historically, but were never known to decline so uniformly worldwide.

Leading Canadian specialist Don Russell, coordinator of a new global network formed to more closely monitor what's happening to the herds, said experts are focusing on "what has changed between this decline and previous declines."

"We've seen a number of areas where climate change is playing a big role, and we see some very dramatic trends," he said in an interview in Whitehorse, the Yukon territorial capital.

In neighboring Northwest Territories, the territorial government on Sept. 24 [2009] reported results of its aerial survey of the Bathurst herd: Its population has dropped to about 32,000, from 128,000 in 2006.

"The numbers are not getting better. There's no good news, no indication of recovery," J. Michael Miltenberger, the environment and natural resources minister, said by telephone from Yellowknife, the capital.

There are probably ominous implications for communities relying on caribou.

He said "there's a huge issue" with the Beverly herd, which numbered 276,000 in 1994, ranging over the Canadian tundra 1,000 miles due north of North Dakota.

"We've been flying north to south, east to west," Miltenberger said. "By our count, with the Beverly herd, they've all but disappeared."

Climate change is piling problem upon problem on the caribou, he said, including bogging them down in thawing permafrost and lengthening the wildfire season, burning up their food.

"The cumulative impact is bringing enormous pressure on the caribou," he said.

And that puts pressure on Canada's "first nations," who for at least 8,000 years have relied on the harvest of caribou meat for the winter larder, have settled along migration routes, have built their material culture around the animal—using skin, bones and sinews for clothing, shelter, tools, thread, even their drums.

"There are probably ominous implications for communities relying on caribou," Russell said.

Such reliance is mirrored in Siberia and northern Scandinavia, where the Sami people make a hard living herding reindeer as livestock. Freezing rains there are reported to have forced Sami to buy fodder to substitute for ice-locked forage.

Easing Hunts

Here in the timeless, silent beauty of Gwich'in country, his people may face "hard decisions," Firth acknowledged, perhaps to limit their hunt to ease the pressure. The Yukon government recently took a first step, restricting hunting to bulls, to spare reproducing cows.

"The future of the Gwich'in and the future of the caribou are the same," the Gwich'in often say. But even more may be at stake.

On this summer day above the Arctic Circle, binoculars found a group of caribou being stalked and circled by a hungry grizzly bear, a needy predator and another link in an intricate, interdependent natural web that may be unraveling, year by year and degree by degree, on the tundra.

8

ANWR Drilling Is Compatible with Caribou Herds and Indigenous Life

Fenton Okomailak Rexford

Fenton Okomailak Rexford is the tribal administrator for the Native Village of Kaktovik, Alaska, and is a member of the Kaktovik City Council. He previously served as the President of Kaktovik Iñupiat Corporation, the titleholder to 92,000 acres of privately owned land within the Coastal Plain of the Arctic National Wildlife Refuge.

The indigenous Iñupiat people of Kaktovik, Alaska, use the lands in and around the Arctic National Wildlife Refuge (ANWR) to support their subsistence lifestyle. The Kaktovik Iñupiat Corporation—a tribal entity—owns 92,000 acres of land in ANWR's Coastal Plain, where oil drilling is proposed. The Iñupiat welcome oil development as a way to stimulate the local economy and pay for basic services that most communities take for granted, such as running water, flush toilets, health clinics, and public high schools. The Iñupiat have very close ties to the land and wildlife and would not favor development if they believed it would harm either of them. The Iñupiat support responsible oil development on the Coastal Plain and believe that it can be done in a way that is environmentally responsible. They do not believe that developing such a small area of land within the massive ANWR region will negatively affect caribou.

Fenton Okomailak Rexford, "Testimony Before the House Committee on Natural Resources, ANWR: Jobs, Energy and Deficit Reduction," *Congressional Quarterly*, September 21, 2011, US House Committee on Natural Resources.

I am a life-long resident of Kaktovik and I intend to grow old there. I can compare what life in Kaktovik was like prior to oil development on the North Slope to the quality of life we have today because of my personal experience. I have spent time listening to the people of Kaktovik and to the residents across the North Slope and the vast majority of us support responsible development of the Coastal Plain of ANWR [Arctic National Wildlife Refuge]. I have had the opportunity to talk to many members of Congress and staff on this issue, with a considerable amount of my time spent in Washington, D.C. I am very familiar with this issue and have been fighting the misrepresentations of the opposition for over 15 years. Therefore, I speak with the institutional knowledge my people, the Iñupiat people of the North Slope, the people who live in the Coastal Plain, have about ANWR.

My people know that industry and wildlife can coexist.

The Coastal Plain of ANWR consists of 1.5 million acres of land and is known as the 1002 area. ANWR itself covers more than 19 million acres of land. The Coastal Plain is a very small portion of this land and, in the pending legislation, Congress proposes to limit development in this area to no more than 2,000 acres—an even smaller portion, less than 0.01% of all of ANWR. We are, therefore, talking about a tiny amount of land within a vast area, most of which is designated as wilderness or refuge. All of this land remains extremely important to the people of Kaktovik and the North Slope Borough. We would not favor development of the Coastal Plain unless we were confident that development can occur without jeopardizing our way of life.

Iñupiat Self-Determination

The Iñupiat people of Kaktovik use the lands in and around ANWR to support our traditional subsistence lifestyle. The land and sea are our gardens and we respect them. We subsist off of the land and sea. As such, we could not support development of the Coastal Plain if it would adversely affect our Iñupiaq traditional subsistence way of life. Responsible development of ANWR's Coastal Plain is a matter of self-determination for my people. It will enable the entire North Slope region continued access to essential services taken for granted by people from the Lower 48.

Over nearly 40 years, we have watched oil development at Prudhoe Bay. Because of this, my people know that industry and wildlife can coexist. The Central Arctic Caribou herd, which calls the Prudhoe Bay region home, numbered around 3,000 in the 1960s. Today the population is thriving at more than 65,000. The Porcupine Caribou Herd in ANWR now numbers about 169,000. We expect this herd to continue to thrive and do not believe that development of such a small area of land within such a massive region will negatively affect these animals. Based on our past experience, we have strong confidence in the North Slope Borough's ability to protect our natural wildlife environment and resources from adverse impact, particularly if decisions are made after considering local input regarding subsistence resources such as caribou.

What Development Will Mean

Responsible ANWR development means my people will continue to have access to running water and flush toilets throughout the region. The luxury of a flush toilet and running water—things we did not have just a few years ago—decreases our risk of exposure to health hazards such as hepatitis. Responsible development also means access to local health care facilities and professionals. Our region is vast and covers roughly 89,000 square miles, yet we have only eight tiny villages. Our only access to a hospital is 360 air miles from Kaktovik to Barrow, with a flight time of 90 minutes, weather permitting. This trip is expensive, particularly for people in an area with little local economy. Responsible development also will continue to support our local health clinics, which are vital to the continued good health of my people.

Development of ANWR also will have important benefits for all Americans.

Further, development of the North Slope enables our community to sustain a local school. For many of my generation, our only option for school beyond eighth grade was to attend an Indian school in the Lower 48. We are now able to provide our children with a high school education on the North Slope.

Finally, responsible development will continue to provide search and rescue, police and fire protection for our North Slope communities. The weather conditions within the North Slope are harsh and at times life threatening. As we continue to practice our traditional subsistence lifestyle, we take comfort in knowing that if we are misguided in our journeys, our region has the capability of conducting search and rescue missions.

ANWR Development Benefits All Americans

Responsible development of ANWR will not just have important benefits for those lucky enough to live on the North Slope. Development of ANWR also will have important benefits for all Americans. In the past few months, many have called for the federal government to reduce its spending deficit, while creating new jobs and stimulating the American economy. Development in ANWR could help to address all three of these concerns.

Opening ANWR to oil and natural gas development would create more than $110 billion in federal revenues and royalties over the next 30 years. North Slope oil development at Prudhoe Bay has already contributed more than $50 billion in federal revenues since 1977. Responsible development on the Coastal Plain would triple that amount. In addition, development of ANWR would result in thousands of new contracts, all across the U.S., for materials and services. The three companies currently producing oil on the North Slope spend money in every one of the 50 states. The additional expenditures related to development of ANWR would in turn create tens of thousands of jobs, many of which could put unemployed Americans back to work in manufacturing facilities, the construction business, and other industries.

National Security and Energy Independence

Also in recent months, Americans have focused on issues of national security, including imported oil and high gasoline prices. Development in ANWR can help resolve these issues, too. Today, we import more than 60% of our oil, much of it from troubled areas in the Middle East. The U.S. Geological Survey [USGS] has repeatedly said that the Coastal Plain represents the best chance for a major oil discovery in the United States. In 1998, the USGS predicted that the Coastal Plain contained 5.7 to 16 billion barrels of recoverable oil. The mean estimate is about 10.4 billions—twice the known oil reserves in Texas or about 30 years of imported oil from Saudi Arabia. The USGS revised its estimate in 2005, predicting that new technologies could significantly increase that amount, while also reducing the footprint of the drilling site and any environmental impacts of drilling. At peak production, ANWR could produce between 650,000 barrels per day and 800,000 barrels per day. This could both reduce our dependence on foreign oil and help reduce gasoline prices. And the more we can reduce the amount of oil produced under troubled, unstable governments, the more our national security would be improved. Development of the Coastal Plain of ANWR is a win-win situation for the American people, particularly for those of use who call this area home.

9

Indigenous Alaskans Support ANWR Drilling

Tara M. Sweeney

Tara M. Sweeney is senior vice president for the Arctic Slope Regional Corporation (ASRC), an Alaska Native corporation formed under the Alaska Native Claims Settlement Act of 1971 for the area that includes the entire North Slope of Alaska. ASRC works to increase the economic and development opportunities within the region, while at the same time preserving Iñupiat culture and traditions.

The indigenous Iñupiat people live on Alaska's North Slope, and the Arctic Slope Regional Corporation represents more than 11,000 Iñupiat shareholders from eight villages in the region. The ASRC owns approximately five million acres of Alaska's North Slope as well as 92,000 subsurface acres of the Coastal Plain area of ANWR, which has been proposed for oil extraction. The Iñupiat support oil development in the area and regard it as an issue of self-determination for the Iñupiat people. The Iñupiat do not believe that oil development would interfere with their traditional way of life, and they say that delays in allowing drilling are detrimental to their community. The Iñupiat call for reforms in the process that allows legal challenges by environmental groups to delay or stop the opening of the area for oil exploration and production.

Tara M. Sweeney, "Testimony on Alaskan Energy for American Jobs Act," US House Committee on Natural Resources, Subcommittee on Energy and Mineral Resources, November 18, 2011.

My name is Tara Sweeney and I am an Iñupiaq Eskimo from Barrow, Alaska. I grew up on the cusp of oil discovery and development in Alaska's Arctic—I remember what it was like as a child to melt ice blocks just to take a bath because we didn't have running water. I was 16 years old when we finally had a flush toilet installed in our house. Advocating for responsible development of the Coastal Plain of ANWR is a second-generation issue for my family.

Today, I serve as the senior vice president of External Affairs for Arctic Slope Regional Corporation, or ASRC, and I am here representing the interests of over 11,000 Iñupiaq shareholders of ASRC.

ASRC is an Alaska Native corporation formed pursuant to the Alaska Native Claims Settlement Act of 1971 (ANCSA) for the area that encompasses the entire North Slope of Alaska. Shareholders of ASRC include nearly all residents of eight villages on the North Slope, Point Hope, Point Lay, Wainwright, Atqasuk, Barrow, Nuiqsut, Kaktovik and Anaktuvuk Pass.

We are committed to increasing the economic and individual development opportunities within our region, and to preserving the Iñupiat culture and traditions. By adhering to the traditional values of protecting the land, the environment, and the culture of the Iñupiat, ASRC has successfully adapted and prospered in an extremely challenging economic climate.

Native Corporation Landholdings

ASRC owns approximately five million acres of land on Alaska's North Slope, conveyed to the corporation under ANCSA, as a settlement of aboriginal land claims. Under the terms of both ANCSA and the Alaska National Interest Lands Conservation Act of 1980 (ANILCA), the unique character of these lands, founded in federal Indian law and the most significant Native claims settlement in U.S. history, must be recognized by Congress and the Federal government in making any land management decisions. ASRC lands are located in areas that either have known resources or are highly prospective for oil, gas, coal, and base minerals. We remain committed to developing these resources and bringing them to market in a manner that respects Iñupiat subsistence values and ensures proper care of the environment, habitat and wildlife.

ASRC and Kaktovik Iñupiat Corporation ("KIC"), the Native Corporation for the Village of Kaktovik, own more than 92,000 subsurface and surface acres, respectively, in the Coastal Plain of the Arctic National Wildlife Refuge, also commonly known as the 1002 Area. These lands hold significant potential for onshore oil and gas development. However, as a result of Section 1003 of ANILCA, these important economic resources remain off limits until further act of Congress, which is why ASRC supports the *Alaskan Energy for American Jobs Act.*

This important piece of legislation asserts Congressional authority to open the Coastal Plain for responsible oil and gas exploration and development, while protecting our Arctic environment. Development of natural resources within wildlife refuges is not uncommon within the United States, even in Alaska.

We would not support development of the Coastal Plain if it had an adverse impact on our ability to feed our families.

Other Alaskan Oilfields

The Kenai National Wildlife Refuge hosted one of Alaska's first oil and gas discoveries and fields, the Swanson River oilfield, discovered in 1959 and produced in 1961. Since the Swanson River field development, there has been a continuous program of exploration and development within the Kenai National Wildlife Refuge. Most recently on November 12, 2011, NordAq Energy announced discovery of a huge gas field in the Kenai National Wildlife Refuge and plans for development are to begin in 2012. NordAq's exploration activities took place on leases from another Alaska Native corporation and occurred within the Kenai National Wildlife Refuge.

Section 1110(b) of ANILCA allows for access to the subsurface in-holdings of another Alaska Native corporation within the Kenai National Wildlife Refuge for exploration, testing and development of hydrocarbons. ASRC has been denied access to our subsurface in-holdings within the Coastal Plain of ANWR, and we desire parity. This legislation aims to afford those same opportunities to ASRC through the repeal of Section 1103 of ANILCA. Further, other national wildlife refuges around the country contain roads, power lines and other infrastructure. We question the differing standard applied to Northern Alaska.

The *Alaskan Energy for American Jobs Act* is aligned with ASRC's mission to enhance Iñupiaq economic opportunities while protecting our cultural and subsistence freedoms through responsible stewardship of our natural environment.

Coastal Plain Is "Home," Not "Wilderness"

The Arctic is an unforgiving climate, home to the Iñupiat, and the only village within the boundaries of ANWR, Kaktovik. The people of Kaktovik, or Qaaktu vigmiut, and the broader North Slope Iñupiat community subsist off the land and the sea. We would not support development of the Coastal Plain if it had an adverse impact on our ability to feed our families the nourishment of caribou, fish, fowl, Dall sheep, musk oxen, moose, or marine mammals.

Some have suggested designating the Coastal Plain as "wilderness", but Iñupiat have called the Coastal Plain home for thousands of years, and we can hardly be considered a "visitor" there. As stated earlier, the area is clearly not one without human habitation. To say that our homelands, where we have lived and that have sustained us for thousands of years, are absent of permanent residents, as if we do not exist—is insulting.

Responsible oil and gas development of the Coastal Plain of ANWR would provide a safe and secure source of energy to the nation, create important jobs for Alaska Natives and throughout the country, and help ensure future flows through the Trans-Alaska Pipeline System, which is now operating at only one-third of its original capacity. With advances in technology, it is possible to develop the Coastal Plain's oil and gas reserves and allow access to much-needed energy resources with minimal land disturbance in the Refuge and without any significant disturbance to wildlife. Technological advances have significantly reduced the "footprint" of oil and gas development. Generally speaking, caribou and other wildlife populations have shown themselves to be highly adaptive to, and have not been adversely affected by, people, machines, and appropriate development (including oil and gas development) in the Refuge or nearby areas.

Energy development anywhere—not just limited to Alaska—is almost always hindered by the threat of litigation.

Several Modifications Are Needed

While we support the *Alaskan Energy for American Jobs Act*, there are several key provisions that ASRC would like to highlight. First, the development and implementation of a competitive oil and gas leasing program within the Coastal Plain. The federal government has taken a bipolar approach to responsible energy development in this country. Elsewhere on the North Slope in the NPR-A [National Petroleum Reserve—Alaska], for example, lands are leased for exploration and never permitted for development, held in limbo by regulatory agency delay. The implementation of a competitive oil and gas leasing program on the Coastal Plain of ANWR is a step closer to increasing domestic oil supply for the benefit of all Americans.

Second, the repeal of Section 1003 ANILCA, which declares that oil and gas leasing program to be compatible with the purposes of ANWR. This is especially important because without this, both ASRC and KIC as private landholders are refugees on our own lands, with no opportunity to responsibly develop resources for the benefit of the North Slope, state of Alaska and the Nation.

Third, we believe it is important under this legislation to maximize Federal revenues by removing any cloud on title and to clarify land ownership with respect to remaining conveyances to ASRC and KIC. It is equally important for ASRC and KIC [to] finalize our lands selections as provided for under PLO 6969 and the 1983 Agreement between ASRC and the United States. We applaud this language to finally fulfill our land selections.

Litigation Safeguards Are Needed

ASRC supports the provisions included in the legislation that address recovery of legal expenses under the *Equal Access to Justice Act*. While the language targets energy legislation, we would support taking it a step further and support including this provision in any legislation regarding energy development, not just energy development in Alaska. Over the past several years we have participated, to various degrees, in efforts to advance exploration and development of energy resources in Alaska. Our experience is that energy development anywhere—not just limited to Alaska—is almost always hindered by the threat of litigation and the ability of third parties to challenge such projects—either administratively or in the courts—regardless of whether the challenges are merited. Unfortunately, in many of these cases third parties can actually recover their costs, including legal fees, even if the challenge is not ultimately successful.

We are concerned that there does not appear to be any mechanism that currently exists to ensure that only legitimate challenges are prosecuted. As a consequence, significant damages can and do occur as a result of delays in the process, even when claims in litigation are ultimately rejected by a court. This currently happens all the time with respect to development in Alaska, and we expect that it will happen even more frequently as efforts continue to develop resources in ANWR, NPR-A, and on the Outer Continental Shelf (OCS).

ASRC stands ready to be part of the domestic energy supply solution.

We urge Congress to consider adopting provisions to ensure that plaintiffs consider the merits of their arguments before they pursue an administrative or judicial challenge to an energy development project. Options could include requiring that such plaintiffs post a bond as part of a challenge to an energy development project, and that they forfeit the bond if their challenge is ultimately unsuccessful. Another option would be legislation that precludes third parties from recovering costs or legal fees—under the *Equal Access to Justice Act* or otherwise—that such third party incurs in bringing a judicial challenge to an energy development project. We are advocating for equitable accountability for all parties who choose to exercise litigious options to delay meaningful energy projects. Project delays of responsible oil and gas development in the Arctic have real-life implications for our people, like threatening the sustainability of providing running water and flush toilets in our communities, local education for our children, or health care facilities, and police and fire protection for our residents.

A Call for Seismic Studies

Finally, in addition to the provisions we support in the *Alaskan Energy for American Jobs Act*, we would like to raise the issue of the necessity of acquiring new seismic data for Coastal Plain resources. Under the Act, future lease sales in the Coastal Plain would necessitate seismic exploration activity to identify areas most promising for recovery of hydrocarbons. While we advocate the opening of the Coastal Plain for leasing we also advocate keeping surface impacts to a minimum. We believe the interest in the hydrocarbon potential under the Coastal Plain could lead to multiple seismic programs in order for companies to collect current data using current technologies for evaluation. We would propose that single seismic be conducted prior to leasing in a manner that allows for community stewardship combined with equipment and procedures focused on assessment with minimal impact of such a program.

It is important to remember that the Coastal Plain of ANWR is the very place that our people have called home since time immemorial, and it continues to provide the resources that support our survival. In addition to the substantial potential value that responsible development of the area's natural resources holds for our people, the land and its resources are essential to our subsistence way of life. It bears repeating that ASRC would not support development of the Coastal Plain if it had an adverse impact on our ability to subsist off the land.

It is incumbent upon Congress to take a leadership role in developing sound energy policy for our nation. The federal government continues to send mixed messages about domestic energy production, and now is the time for Congress to act in the best interests of Americans with respect to domestic energy and energy supply. ASRC stands ready to be part of the domestic energy supply solution for Congress.

10

Dances with Ghosts

Dennis J. Kucinich

Dennis J. Kucinich is the US Representative for Ohio's tenth congressional district. He was a candidate for the Democratic nomination for President of the United States in the 2004 and 2008 presidential elections.

For hundreds of years, the United States's relationship with our native peoples has been one of exploitation. The country needs to change this cycle by prohibiting drilling in the Arctic National Wildlife Refuge (ANWR). Drilling in ANWR would threaten the way of life of the Gwich'in tribe by disrupting caribou calving grounds, leading to the long-term decline of the herd and the Gwich'in people that depend upon them for survival. Drilling in ANWR is damaging, not just to Alaska and the Gwich'in tribe, but to ourselves as humans, as well as the legacy we leave behind.

Early in the morning on Monday, December 19, the United States House of Representatives will vote on the Defense Authorization bill, which contains a provision to permit the drilling for oil in the Arctic National Wildlife Refuge (ANWR).

I have taken three opportunities on the floor of the House early today to alert the American people of this back-door approach to passing a very controversial bill, which is desecration of the basic human rights of the Gwich'in people. When will America get off the treadmill of sacrificing native rights to greed, territorial ambitions and fear? We will soon observe a grim anniversary that testifies to our persistent moral dilemma when it comes to those who were here first.

One hundred and fifteen years ago, on December 29, 1890, the US Seventh Calvary, under the control of Col. James Forsyth, directed artillery fire against Lakota men, women and children. One hundred and fifty Native Americans were killed in what became known as the Massacre at Wounded Knee in South Dakota. US government troops were drawn to the land of the Lakotas to enforce a ban on Ghost Dance Religion, a native mysticism that taught nonviolence and included chanting prayers and dancing through which one could achieve the ecstasy of harmony with the paradise of the natural world.

The dance was forbidden out of fear that excitation of religious passions would turn to Indian violence against the US government. The history of the United States's relationship with our native peoples has been one shame-ridden chapter after another of expropriation, humiliation and deception, theft of lands, theft of natural resources, destruction of sacred sites and massacres. The United States's relationship with our native peoples has been an endless cycle of exploitation and contrition, massacres and apologies.

When we perpetrate acts of violence, such as drilling in ANWR, we are damaging ourselves as humans.

Who in the future United States will apologize to the descendants of today's Gwich'in tribe, whose humble, natural way of life, religion and culture are threatened with extinction by the plan to drill oil in the Arctic National Wildlife Refuge? The Gwich'in tribe has lived on its ancestral lands for 20,000 years in harmony with the natural world. The drilling for oil in the coastal plain of the Arctic Refuge, called by the Gwich'in "the Sacred Place Where All Life Begins," will disrupt caribou calving grounds, leading to the long-term decline not only of the herd but of the tribe that depends upon it for survival.

This will not only violate internationally recognized human rights of the Gwich'in; it will also make a mockery of our founding principles of belief in the inalienable right of each person to "life, liberty and pursuit of happiness." Members of Congress will come to the floor today and say we need to drill to protect our economy, to defend our country, to keep our way of life.

I intend to point to the reciprocal nature of our moral decisions. Christian teaching tells us to do unto others as we would have them do unto ourselves. We learn from other spiritual insights that what we do unto others we actually do to ourselves. We cannot in the consciousness of true American spirit return to a history of slavery, a history where women had no rights or a history where native peoples are objectified and deprived of their humanity, their culture, their religion, their health, their lives. We must make our stand now not only as to who the Gwich'in are but, in a world where all are interdependent and interconnected, who we are and what we will become based on our decisions today.

When we perpetrate acts of violence, such as drilling in ANWR, we are damaging ourselves as humans. It destroys the land, it destroys the herd, it destroys the Gwich'in. It destroys us all. Another part of the true America will die. We must not only search for alternative energy. We must search for an alternative way to live. We must escape this cycle of destruction. We must reconcile with nature. We must find a path to peace, with our native brothers and sisters and with ourselves.

One hundred and fifteen years ago, the Ghost Dancers were killed. Yet we still meet their ghosts. They are dancing upon the coastal plains of the Arctic National Wildlife Refuge.

11

ANWR Drilling Would Create Jobs and Jumpstart the Economy

Sean Parnell

Republican Sean Parnell is the governor of the state of Alaska.

Producing more domestic energy is the best way for America to improve its economy, and oil production in the Arctic National Wildlife Refuge (ANWR) is the best way to do it. Drilling for oil in ANWR will create jobs and stimulate not just the local Alaskan economy but the national economy as well. This is because as more oil becomes available, oil prices decline and the cost of doing business declines right along with it. Those savings, in turn, create more demand for goods and services, which again means more job creation. In addition, ANWR oil would decrease the trade deficit, generate billions in federal revenues and help protect the Trans Alaska Pipeline system, a critical piece of the country's energy infrastructure. It is time to start drilling and bring ANWR oil to America.

In Alaska, we set a goal to increase the throughput of the Trans Alaska Pipeline System (TAPS) to one million barrels a day from current levels of about 550,000 barrels per day. I have asked other governors to set increasing production goals, as well.

Sean Parnell, "Testimony Before the House Committee on Natural Resources, ANWR: Jobs, Energy and Deficit Reduction," US House Committee on Natural Resources, September 21, 2011.

This will help grow our nation's economy, make us more energy secure, and more energy dependent.

Reaching this goal of a million barrels per day through TAPS will take work between the federal government and the State of Alaska, where each owns substantial oil and gas resources.

The task before us all is to create jobs, to grow our economy.

To boil it down to one simple truth: More American oil and gas production means jobs. And jobs translate into stable communities, and a strong nation.

Beyond the Beltway [Washington, DC], Americans believe that our nation faces an almost insurmountable debt burden, leading some to ask if it is even possible to pay it down, given our current GDP [gross domestic product].

Many thoughtful Americans are alarmed at the nearly $15 trillion federal debt, and they worry about the future of our great nation.

And yet, we can regain our economic footing through producing more American energy.

This transition to renewables cannot take place all at once.

America's workforce wins, families win, job creators win, and the federal government wins—more revenue.

Look at the states doing relatively well in this economic downturn: They are America's major energy-producers. Alaska is one of those states. Yet, we are held back from contributing more affordable energy to other Americans by federal regulators who want to keep federal lands off limits to oil and gas exploration.

Bringing All Resources into Play

America is blessed with natural resources, both renewable and non-renewable. We need them all right now.

This transition to renewables cannot take place all at once. That's like going from first gear to fifth gear—you risk stalling the engine of our economy by starving it of power.

And some of our nation's richest oil reserves exist along the coastal plain known as ANWR [Arctic National Wildlife Refuge].

It's accessible. It's extractable. And oil production and wildlife in ANWR are compatible.

Oil from ANWR could help meet U.S. demand for the next 25 years—or longer.

Responsible development of ANWR would create hundreds of thousands of jobs across our nation, in virtually every state, because a secure supply of petroleum will create demand for goods and services, and lower the cost of doing business.

As you know, the United States imports over 65 percent of our nation's annual petroleum needs. These imports cost more than $150 billion a year. That figure does not include the military costs—and the human cost—of imported oil, which is truly incalculable.

What is the resource we call ANWR? And in such a remote location on Alaska's northern edge, how did we first learn that oil was even present?

Protecting the environment is as important to Alaskans as it is to all Americans.

The U.S. Geological Survey estimates that the amount of technically recoverable oil beneath the coastal plain ranges between 5.7 billion and nearly 16 billion barrels. Studies suggest the coastal plain could produce a 10-year sustained rate of one million barrels per day.

ANWR is a 19-million-acre national wildlife refuge. This national refuge is approximately the size of South Carolina. However, exploration and production can come from only a small part of ANWR known as the Coastal Plain of ANWR.

Coastal Plain Potential

The Coastal Plain was designated by Congress in 1980 as requiring special study to determine its oil and gas potential and the effects of development on the environment. In 1987, the Department of the Interior recommended development.

Today's technology ensures that the footprint for development in ANWR would be less than 2,000 acres—approximately half the size of Andrews Air Force Base [in Maryland] (4,320 acres) in a land mass the size of South Carolina. Additionally, technology now allows for almost "zero impact exploration" through the use of ice roads, ice pads, and the like.

Protecting the environment is as important to Alaskans as it is to all Americans. This Great Land is our home, and we have to be good stewards of air, land, and sea to live here.

For most of the year, the Coastal Plain is frozen. It has low biological activity. Experience shows that seasonal restrictions and other environmental stipulations can be used to protect caribou during their six-week calving season each summer.

Appropriate restrictions can also protect migratory birds and fish. Our experience with other North Slope fields shows it can be done.

Prudhoe Bay, for example, located 60 miles west of ANWR, has been operating for over 30 years and has produced more than 16 billion barrels of oil so far. Amidst that, the Central Arctic caribou herd at Prudhoe Bay has grown from 5,000 in 1975 to over 67,000 in 2008.

The Trans Alaska Pipeline System is a world class oil transportation system and one of this nation's most significant and valuable assets. Every day, Alaska oil moves through TAPS to refineries in Washington State and in California.

But declining production from Alaska's fields is taking its toll on TAPS.

The Pipeline Needs Oil

The Trans Alaska Pipeline is not designed to flow at low rates. Below 550,000 barrels per day, the risk of clogs and corrosion increase. The very real possibility of a mid-winter shut down is an urgent concern.

A reserve of Alaska oil locked in the ground makes no sense when Americans need jobs and our economy needs a jump start.

Bringing new production from ANWR and other Alaska fields is critical to preserve this valuable piece of our nation's infrastructure. Without increased production, our economy is at greater risk as is our national security.

With oil from ANWR in the Trans Alaska Pipeline, it will be feasible to develop other marginal fields that otherwise might not be economic. It's all about growing jobs and our economy, and about keeping America safe.

The Coastal Plain of ANWR is America's best bet for the discovery of another giant "Prudhoe Bay-sized" oil and gas field in North America. Many economic benefits would result, not the least of which are the federal revenues that would be in the billions of dollars.

But a reserve of Alaska oil locked in the ground makes no sense when Americans need jobs and our economy needs a jump start that government is impotent to provide.

If the federal government persists in blocking oil development in Alaska, it could mean the dismantling of the Alaska pipeline, and the stranding of every last bit of oil that exists in our Arctic.

It's Time to Bring ANWR Oil to America

For millions of Americans out of work and struggling to make ends meet, federal regulatory policy blocking oil development only deepens the wounds. In Alaska, the federal administration has blocked exploration in ANWR, has blocked exploration in NPR-A [National Petroleum Reserve–Alaska], and has blocked exploration in the Arctic offshore.

When it comes to ANWR, we've heard people say that it will not impact the price of fuel now, because it will take too long to bring online. They've been saying that for 20 years. That's a disingenuous argument.

It's time to reduce dependence on oil from unstable, unfree, and unfriendly regions of the world.

Bring ANWR oil to America, and decrease the trade deficit.

Bring ANWR oil to America, and increase American jobs.

Bring ANWR oil to America, and reduce the federal debt with revenues and taxes from a more vibrant economy.

12

ANWR Drilling Would Violate Human Rights

Sarah Agnus James

Sarah Agnus James is Neetsa'ii Gwich'in from Arctic Village, Alaska. She serves as chairperson of the Gwich'in Steering Committee, an indigenous group founded in 1988 to oppose oil exploration in the Arctic National Wildlife Refuge.

A representative of the indigenous Gwich'in people testified before the House Committee on Natural Resources in November 2011, arguing that oil development in the Arctic National Wildlife Refuge (ANWR) would violate the basic human rights of the Gwich'in people. The Gwich'in call the Coastal Plain of ANWR, where drilling is proposed, the "Sacred Place Where Life Begins" because that is where the Porcupine caribou herd has its calving grounds. The lives of the Gwich'in are inextricably linked to the caribou, which they use for food, tools, shelter, and religious and cultural reasons. Any disruption to the caribou will also disrupt the traditional lifeways of the Gwich'in. The International Covenant on Civil and Political Rights, signed by the president and ratified by the US Senate, states that "in no case may a people be deprived of their own means of subsistence," which the Gwich'in believe would be the case if ANWR oil is developed.

The Gwich'in are caribou people. Caribou is our main food, it is in our tools and clothes and songs and stories and beadwork. We have lived right here with the caribou for

Sara Agnus James, "Testimony Before the House Committee on Natural Resources, ANWR: Jobs, Energy and Deficit Reduction," US House Committee on Natural Resources, November 18, 2011.

hundreds of generations and will stay right [here] far into the future. There are maybe 7,000 of us, mostly living in 15 small communities and villages scattered across northeast Alaska and the northwest corner of Canada. We are among the most remote and most traditional people in America.

The Gwich'in Steering Committee was created by resolution of our Chiefs in 1988 at the first gathering of all our people in more than 100 years—the Gwich'in Niintsyaa. Our job is to speak with one voice for all our Gwich'in people on the caribou issue. The Chiefs gave us two directions:

- to tell the world about the caribou and the Gwich'in way of life, and what oil development would mean for the Gwich'in; and

- to do it in a good way.

So, Mr. Chairman, I am especially honored to be here today to carry out this important task for my Chiefs and my people.

Oil development in the Arctic National Wildlife Refuge is not just about money and oil. It is about the most basic human rights of the Gwich'in.

Gwich'in See Both Sides

We respect the difficult job you have. We know about the problems of jobs and energy. In Arctic Village we only have jobs in the summer, and there are not enough to go around, so we know what it is like to be unemployed and to worry about how to pay our bills. We also know about energy problems. In Arctic Village everything is flown in. If you have a 4-wheeler or snow-machine, you will pay about $15/gallon for gas. Fuel for electric generators is flown in too, so electricity is really expensive. I'm not complaining, I love my life, but we do know what it means to have a "deficit" when life is expensive. But in the winter you can't just turn out the lights. You have to get the money to pay the bills. Go to town to get a job, or raise taxes. You have to keep the lights on at home.

The idea of waiting to pay the bills for 10 or 15 years while you hope to find oil in the Arctic Wildlife Refuge is backwards. People need to go to work now. Our country, our government needs to fix our schools and roads and towns, and find a way to meet new needs like icebreakers—not 10 or 20 years from now, but now. If it costs more money, we will pay our fair share. To go on pretending you can just cut costs without ruining our country is not telling the truth.

But the question of oil development in the Arctic National Wildlife Refuge is not just about money and oil. It is about the most basic human rights of the Gwich'in.

For the Gwich'in, this is a simple issue:

Oil development in the birthplace and nursery grounds of the Porcupine (River) Caribou Herd would hurt the caribou and threaten the culture and way of life of my people and the viability of our communities.

If the caribou are disturbed they have nowhere to go.

"The Sacred Place Where Life Begins"

We know the coastal plain of the Arctic National Wildlife Refuge as *Iizhik Gwats'an Gwandaii Goodlit*, "the Sacred Place Where Life Begins." After migrating 400 miles and giving birth, the mother caribou cannot be disturbed at this time, and our people may not go there then. The cows and their calves will move from place to place to find the cotton-grass and other new green sprouts they need to recover their strength and feed their calves. Depending on weather, the prime area for feeding might change from year to year, especially for the first weeks. Sometimes when snows are deep the caribou are born in Canada, but studies of radio-collared caribou show that as soon as she can, the mother caribou will lead her calf onto the Arctic Refuge's coastal plain. From what we know, every Porcupine caribou gets their start in life right there, at *Iizhik Gwats'an Gwandaii Goodlit.*

When oil development around Prudhoe Bay came close to the calving grounds of the Central Arctic Caribou Herd, the cows and their calves were pushed away onto new calving- and nursery grounds. Because there was lots of good ground, this did not hurt them and those caribou prospered.

The problem for Porcupine caribou is, in the Arctic Refuge the mountains come close to the Arctic Ocean—and the coastal plain is only a few miles wide. There are already more caribou per square mile on the Porcupine caribou calving and nursery grounds than almost any other caribou herd. If the caribou are disturbed they have nowhere to go. Caribou biologists believe oil development, or any large-scale disturbance and noise, risks displacement of cow and calve caribou from essential habitats, would likely hurt productivity, leading to declines, and possibly alter migration patterns.

These are the expected and unavoidable effects of oil development even if it is done right. This is not the risk we face if there is a spill or other large industrial accident.

The Rights of Indigenous People

As indigenous people, we have the right to continue our way of life, and that right is guaranteed by the International Covenant on Civil and Political Rights, signed by the President and Ratified by the Senate. Article 1 of that Covenant reads in part:

"In no case may a people be deprived of their own means of subsistence."

The U.S. and Canadian governments signed an international agreement for management and long-term protection of the Porcupine Caribou Herd (Ottawa, July 17, 1987), forming the International Porcupine Caribou Commission (IPCC).

The objectives of the agreement were: "To conserve the Porcupine Caribou Herd and its habitat through international cooperation and coordination so that the risk of irreversible damage or long-term adverse effects as a result of use of caribou or their habitat is minimized; To ensure opportunities for *customary and traditional uses of the Porcupine Caribou Herd* (emphasis added); To enable users of Porcupine Caribou to participate in the international coordination of the conservation of the Porcupine Caribou Herd and its habitat; To encourage cooperation [and] communication among governments, users of Porcupine Caribou and others to achieve these objectives."

It is the very simple human right to continue to live our lives on our traditional lands that I hope you will remember.

Wording of Agreement Supports Cause

Much of the language used in this international (governments-to-governments) agreement admits and supports the Gwich'in human and cultural rights regarding caribou habitat:

- "Acknowledging that there are various human uses of caribou and that for generations certain people of Yukon Territory and the Northwest Territories in Canada have customarily and traditionally harvested Porcupine Caribou to meet their nutritional, cultural and other essential needs and will continue to do so in the future . . . and that these people should participate in the conservation of the Porcupine Caribou Herd and its habitat;"

- "Recognizing that . . . caribou in their large free-roaming herds comprise a unique and irreplaceable natural resource of great value which each generation should maintain ... so as to conserve them for future generations;"

- "... actions for the conservation of the Porcupine Caribou Herd that result in the long-term detriment of other indigenous species of wild fauna and flora should be avoided;"

- [referencing territory covered] "... caribou found north of 64 degrees, 30' north latitude and north of the Yukon River which usually share common and traditional calving and post-calving aggregation grounds between the Canning River in the State of Alaska and the Babbage River in Yukon Territory and which historically migrate within the State of Alaska, Yukon Territory, and the Northwest Territories;"

- [under 'Objectives'] "f. The Parties should avoid or minimize activities that would significantly disrupt migration or other important behavior patterns of the Porcupine Caribou Herd or that would otherwise lessen the ability of users of Porcupine Caribou to use the Herd."

There are other documents that support our claim, but it is the very simple human right to continue to live our lives on our traditional lands that I hope you will remember.

13

ANWR Drilling Footprint Would Be Insignificant

Mark Hyman

Mark Hyman is an award-winning commentator who appears on television news stations for Sinclair Broadcast Group.

Environmentalists who oppose oil exploration have long portrayed the Arctic National Wildlife Refuge (ANWR) as a place of supreme beauty, filled with abundant wildlife, rich flora, and spectacular scenery. This image of ANWR is only partially true; in actuality the specific area proposed for drilling is stark, barren, and little used by animals. Moreover, that area is such a miniscule part of the overall Refuge that some have described it as a "postage stamp on a football field" or a "pencil dot on a full piece of paper." A congressional delegation visited the area on a fact-finding mission in 2008 and documented the desolate conditions on video, in the hopes of countering the misleading images of the place. The impact of drilling in such a tiny and barren area would be insignificant and would not adversely affect the Arctic National Wildlife Refuge as a whole.

The term ANWR, the abbreviation for the Arctic National Wildlife Refuge, has been thrust into the lexicon of daily American use in light of increased global energy demands and soaring energy costs at home. ANWR has become the Maginot Line [a line of obstacles and defences built by the French prior to WWII to defend their borders with Germany and

Italy] for environmentalists and their Congressional supporters. Environmentalists have successfully fought a nearly three-decade long battle to prohibit drilling for oil in the petroleum-rich region. The entire refuge has been portrayed as an idyllic slice of American wilderness filled with colorful fauna, grazing wildlife, and babbling brooks nestled among majestic mountains. This caricature has all of the trappings of a Disney movie backdrop.

ANWR does include some of those splendorous images—and a bit of everything else. At about 19.5 million acres, ANWR is the size of the state of South Carolina. Located in Alaska's northeast corner and stretching from that state's northern coast along the frigid Arctic Ocean to two hundred miles south, ANWR includes a broad spectrum of Alaskan wilderness. The spectacular geography of the southern three-quarters of ANWR is offset by the flat, barren and desolate northern slope along the coast. The two contrasting landscapes are separated by the Brooks Mountain Range running east and west.

"A Postage Stamp on a Football Field"

The section of ANWR known as Area 10-02 is about 1.2 million acres in size and includes a sliver of about 2,000 acres identified for oil extraction. "It is the equivalent," said Craig Williams, "of a postage stamp on a football field." Williams graduated from high school in Alaska and has family that lives in the state, but he now lives in Pennsylvania. A candidate for Pennsylvania's 7th Congressional District, Williams and six other U.S. House candidates traveled to ANWR and the neighboring region on July 15–16 [2008] to get a first-hand look at the subject of so much controversy.

Area 10-02 got its name from section 1002 of the "Alaska National Interest Lands Conservation Act," legislation passed and signed into law in December 1980 by a lame duck Congress and President Jimmy Carter, following the landslide victory by Ronald Reagan. The Act set aside more than 75 million acres of Alaska territory as federally protected public lands in order to prevent state and local development. Section 1002 specifically established the guidelines for oil exploration in the region.

Joining Williams were congressional candidates Paul Stark (Wisconsin-3), Luke Puckett (Indiana-2), Greg Goode (Indiana-8), Mike Sodrel (Indiana-9), Chris Lien (South Dakota-AL), and Jason Chaffetz (Utah-3). Five of the seven are challenging incumbent members of Congress who vehemently oppose developing oil excavation in Area 10-02. Chaffetz is running for a vacant seat after defeating incumbent Chris Cannon in the Republican primary and Puckett's opponent, Rep. Joe Donnelly, recently abandoned his opposition to ANWR drilling.

Oil workers are fined if they violate any rules that safeguard the environment or the wildlife.

A Factfinding Mission to ANWR

The logistics involved in traveling to ANWR were very complicated, underscoring the remoteness of the region. Adrian Herrera, an Alaskan official with the not-for-profit group Arctic Power, helped plan the trip. Hiring a private aircraft to complete the journey and survey Area 10-02 was a virtual necessity, without having to resort to a multi-day, rugged overland trip.

The congressional candidates also visited Prudhoe Bay, approximately 75 miles to the west of Area 10-02 and the site of the existing Alaska oil pipeline that would be used to carry ANWR oil. Oil excavation has been under way in Prudhoe Bay since 1977. The men wanted to inspect a current oil drilling operation to see if it was the ecological disaster environmentalists claim will befall Area 10-02.

"There was no environmental degradation. The area was pristine," said Stark. "I was impressed with the care the oil companies undertake to protect the environment. They even place giant diapers under the vehicles in order to capture anything that could possibly fall." Oil drilling is conducted only in the winter using ice roads in order not to disturb the tundra. There are no roads to many of the facilities during the non-winter months.

Environmental Stewardship

According to Stark, oil workers are fined if they violate any rules that safeguard the environment or the wildlife, such as not bringing a vehicle to a complete stop and turning off the engine if caribou are present. A second violation brings immediate dismissal.

Suggestions that 10-02 is an area rich in wildlife and abundant vegetation are flat-out wrong.

Williams was similarly impressed in spite of confiding that he was a bit skeptical before he made the trip. What he witnessed was more remarkable than what he had anticipated. "These people are responsible stewards of the environment," he said. Williams noted that the latest technology will allow ANWR drilling to occupy a significantly smaller area of land than the 1970s technology that was used to develop Prudhoe Bay. "The footprint is tiny, truly tiny," he said. "It is pencil dot on full page of paper."

Leaseholders BP Oil and Conoco-Phillips are currently pumping 750,000 barrels each day (from a 1980s high of two million barrels daily) from the Prudhoe Bay fields, with a reserve estimated to have been in excess of 15 billion barrels. Area 10-02 is believed to hold even larger petroleum reserves.

Suggestions that 10-02 is an area rich in wildlife and abundant vegetation are flat-out wrong, observed Herrera. "Tenoh-two is located along the coastal plain, north of the Brooks Mountain Range. It is flat and the actual ground is peat tundra," said Herrera. "There are no trees and no permanent wildlife. The caribou do not have regular migratory patterns. They have passed through the area four times in the last ten years. It is rather desolate."

The Local Lifestyle

The only settlement in Area 10-02 is the City of Kaktovik, situated about 150 miles to the east of Prudhoe Bay. Kaktovik is an island community of about 280 native Kaktovikmiut people (often referred to as "Inuit") just off the mainland in the Arctic Ocean. The lifestyle in Kaktovik is harsh by any standard. Kaktovik acquired running water and flush toilets only four years ago. Winter lasts for eight months. Nearly three of those months the area is plunged into total darkness. Summer is fleeting, lasting only about six weeks. The Area 10-02 tundra sits on hundreds of feet of permafrost. It is not the beautiful landscape described by environmental activists and their Congressional backers.

According to Herrera, ANWR opponents show photographs of the Brooks Mountains located about 45 miles to the south of the area identified for oil drilling in an apparent attempt to misrepresent the true geographic nature of the area.

As measured by the public outcry, political opposition to domestic oil production has become increasingly untenable.

The delegation freely questioned villagers in Kaktovik and Barrow, a village of about 4,000 people located nearly 300 miles to the west of Area 10-02, and the county headquarters of the North Slope Borough, the local government entity encompassing Alaska's north slope. "We did not meet a single villager or local official opposed to drilling in the area," reported Stark.

The Kaktovik villagers view ANWR drilling as critical to the continuation of their lifestyle. They are shareholders of 92,000 acres in ANWR, including the subterranean mineral rights. Drilling will bring in much-needed revenue to their ancestral area that is plagued by astronomical prices due to the village's remoteness. A homebuilder by profession, Stark was informed it costs more than $300,000 to build a 1,000 square foot home due to high material and labor costs. Villagers are anxious to build a new school with ANWR royalties.

A Picture Is Worth a Thousand Words

The traveling contingent hired a professional video photographer to record their trip and interviews. They intend to make the video available in the days ahead. At a July 17 [2008] press conference in Anchorage to report their findings, the seven congressional candidates were joined by Alaska Governor Sarah Palin and Lieutenant Governor Sean Parnell.

The worldwide demand for energy has squeezed oil supplies and has led to skyrocketing fuel costs. As measured by the public outcry, political opposition to domestic oil production has become increasingly untenable. The absurdity of efforts to prevent drilling in the U.S. is highlighted by a House bill passed in May [2008] that would have the Justice Department sue OPEC [Organization of Petroleum Exporting Countries] nations for not producing more oil to meet U.S. needs. ANWR opponents believe other countries have an obligation to do exactly what they oppose the U.S. could be doing at home. The political left's long discredited cry of "No blood for oil!" could be replaced with "Let's sue for oil!" Video recordings and first-hand observations offered by Williams and the others will likely increase public pressure on Congressional Democrats who oppose Area 10-02 oil excavation.

14

Major Oil Spill in Alaska: Congress Eyes ANWR as Oil Spills in the Arctic

Jason Leopold

Jason Leopold is the author of the memoir News Junkie.

Drilling for oil in the Arctic National Wildlife Refuge (ANWR) cannot be done in an environmentally sensitive way. Current BP operations in Alaska are deeply flawed and already place the environment at risk. Dysfunctional safety valves at the Prudhoe Bay oil fields, which would be duplicated at ANWR, increase the potential for oil spills and would be further environmentally devastating. Although oil company executives have downplayed the severity of these technological problems, BP whistleblowers have urged Congress to investigate. Oil development has also created havoc with the traditional lifestyles of the Gwich'in people, in addition to pollution and displacing wildlife. We should protect our natural resources. For this reason, the United States should not open the Arctic National Wildlife Refuge for drilling.

With its March passage of a budget measure, the US Senate approved a provision to open up the Arctic National Wildlife Refuge to drilling—just as the region suffers one of the worst oil spills in its history.

The provision to permit drilling in ANWR was included in a resolution passed by the Senate Budget Committee. The full Senate is expected to vote on the issue before press time.

The measure was prepared by the Republican-controlled Senate in such a way that it would be protected from a filibuster by Senate Democrats opposed to it. Drilling in ANWR has been debated at least half a dozen times over the past five years.

The issue is a cornerstone of President Bush's National Energy Policy. Bush claims that drilling in ANWR is crucial in order for the US to cut its dependence on foreign oil.

Environmentalists and numerous lawmakers have derided the plan, saying it would lead to the destruction of caribou and other wildlife that live in the refuge. Moreover, severe safety and technological issues have plagued the big oil companies that drill in nearby Prudhoe Bay and that would be responsible for breaking ground in ANWR should the Senate measure pass.

Because the companies have yet to take measures to address the safety issues at their Prudhoe Bay operations and make much-needed technological upgrades, there have been dozens of oil spills in the area. The situation would likely become even worse if ANWR were to be opened up to exploration, according to environmental officials and activist groups.

In March, the worst spill in the history of oil development in Alaska's North Slope forced the closing of five oil processing centers in the region. Alaskan state officials said that as much as 260,000 gallons of crude oil leaking out of a pipeline in an oil field jointly owned by Exxon Mobil, BP, and Conoco-Phillips blanketed two acres of frozen tundra near Prudhoe Bay—just a short distance from where President Bush has proposed opening up ANWR to drilling.

The oil spill went undetected for about five days before an oilfield worker noticed the scent of hydrocarbons while driving through the area on March 2, leading him to believe there was a spill from one of the facilities.

It's expected that the spill will take a crew of 60 at least two weeks to clean up and to restore crude production to pre-spill levels. The petroleum processing centers will remain closed until then.

The spill underscores the hazards of drilling in the Arctic, despite the fact that oil company executives have downplayed the severity of the technological problems likely to be associated with it.

Last year, unbeknownst to the federal lawmakers who debated the merits of drilling in ANWR, the Alaska Department of Environmental Conservation started laying the groundwork to pursue civil charges against BP and the corporation's drilling contractor for failing to report massive oil spills at its Prudhoe Bay operation, located just 60 miles west of ANWR.

Despite those dire warnings, neither Congress nor the Senate has shown interest in investigating the whistleblowers' claims, nor held hearings about the potential problems that could result from drilling in ANWR.

But BP employees have warned lawmakers that oil spills like the one that took place in March could happen in ANWR if upgrades aren't made to the oil companies' drilling equipment.

In March of 2002, a BP whistleblower went public with his claims of maintenance backlogs and employee shortages at BP's Prudhoe Bay operations that he said could become even worse if ANWR is opened up to exploration.

BP has long been criticized for poorly managing the North Slope's aging pipelines.

The whistleblower, Robert Brian, who worked as an instrument technician at Prudhoe Bay for 22 years, had a lengthy meeting with aides to Senators Joseph Lieberman and Bob Graham, both Democrats, to discuss his claims. But the senators have never followed up on that.

At the time, Brian said he supported opening up ANWR to oil exploration but said BP has imperiled that goal because it is "putting Prudhoe workers and the environment at risk."

"We are trying to change that so we don't have a catastrophe that ends up on CNN and stops us from getting into ANWR," he said, according to a March 13, 2002, report in the Anchorage Daily News.

BP has long been criticized for poorly managing the North Slope's aging pipelines, safety valves and other critical components of its oil production infrastructure.

The company has in the past made minor improvements to its valves and fire detection systems and hired additional employees but has neglected to maintain a level of safety at its facilities on the North Slope.

Chuck Hamel, a highly regarded activist who is credited with exposing dozens of oil spills and the subsequent cover-ups related to BP's shoddy operations at Prudhoe Bay, sent a letter to Senator Pete Domenici (R-NM) on April 15, 2005, saying the senator was duped by oil executives and state officials during a recent visit to Alaska's North Slope.

"You obviously are unaware of the cheating by some producers and drilling companies," Hamel said in the letter to Domenici, an arch-proponent of drilling in ANWR. "Your official Senate tour [of Alaska last March] was masked by the orchestrated 'dog and pony show' provided you at the new Alpine Field, away from the real world of the Slope's dangerously unregulated operations."

Back in the 1980s, Hamel was the first person to expose weak pollution laws at the Valdez tanker port as well as electrical and maintenance problems with the trans-Alaska oil pipeline.

Hamel has said that not only do oil spills continue on the North Slope because BP neglects to address maintenance issues, but the oil behemoth's executives have routinely lied to

Alaskan state representatives and members of the United States Senate and Congress about the steps they're taking to correct the problems.

Hamel has obtained some damning evidence on BP to back up his claims. He has photographs showing oil wells spewing a brown substance known as drilling mud, which contains traces of crude oil, on two separate occasions.

Hamel says he's determined to expose BP's shoddy operations and throw a wrench in President Bush's plans to open up ANWR to drilling.

"Contrary to what President Bush has been saying, the current BP Prudhoe Bay operations—particularly the dysfunctional safety valves—are deeply flawed and place the environment, the safety of the operations staff and the integrity of the facility at risk. The president should delay legislation calling for drilling at the Arctic National Wildlife Refuge," Hamel told the *Wall Street Journal* last year.

In April of 2001, whistleblowers informed Hamel and former Interior Secretary Gale Norton, who at the time was touring the Prudhoe Bay oil fields, that the safety valves at Prudhoe Bay, which kick in in the event of a pipeline rupture, failed to close. Secondary valves that connect the oil platforms with processing plants also failed to close. And because the technology at Prudhoe Bay would be duplicated at ANWR, the potential for a massive explosion and huge spills are very real.

"A major spill or fire at one of our [processing centers] will exit the piping at high pressure, and leave a half-mile-wide oil slick on the white snow," Hamel said at the time in an interview with the *Wall Street Journal*.

That year, the Alaska Oil and Gas Conservation Commission found high failure rates on some Prudhoe wellhead safety valves. The company was put on federal criminal probation after one of its contractors dumped thousands of gallons of toxic material underground at BP's Endicott oil field in the

1990s. BP pleaded guilty to the charges in 2000 and paid a $6.5 million fine, and agreed to set up a nationwide environmental management program that has cost more than $20 million.

Hamel also claimed that whistleblowers had told of another cover-up, dating back to 2003, in which Pioneer Natural Resources and its drilling contractor, Nabors Alaska Drilling, allegedly disposed of more than 2,000 gallons of toxic drilling mud and fluids through the ice "to save the cost of proper disposal on shore."

Hamel has had his share of detractors, notably BP executives and several Alaskan state officials, as well as the federal EPA, who have branded him a conspiracy theorist.

But last March, Hamel was vindicated when Alaska's Department of Environmental Conservation confirmed his claims of major spills in July 2003 and December 2004 at the oil well owned by BP and operated by its drilling contractor, Nabors, on the North Slope, which the company had never reported as required by state law.

No one can tell us that opening the Arctic Refuge to development can be done in an environmentally sensitive way with a small footprint. It cannot be done.

Hamel filed a formal complaint in January 2005 with the EPA, claiming he had pictures showing a gusher spewing a brown substance. An investigation by Alaska's Department of Environmental Conservation determined that as much as 294 gallons of drilling mud was spilled when gas was sucked into wells, causing sprays of drilling mud and oil that shot up as high as 85 feet into the air.

Because both spills exceeded 55 gallons, BP and Nabors were obligated under a 2003 compliance agreement that BP signed with Alaska to immediately report the spills. That didn't occur, said Leslie Pearson, the agency's spill prevention and emergency response manager.

President Bush has said that the oil and gas industry can open up ANWR without damaging the environment or displacing wildlife. But the native Gwich'in Nation, in Alaska for centuries, whose 7,000 members make their living in Alaska's oil country say President Bush is wrong.

"Existing oil development has displaced caribou, polluted the air and water and created havoc with the traditional lifestyles of the people," said Jonathan Solomon, chairman of the Gwich'in Steering Committee, in a May 7, 2005, interview with the *Financial Times*. "No one can tell us that opening the Arctic Refuge to development can be done in an environmentally sensitive way with a small footprint. It cannot be done."

Organizations to Contact

The editors have compiled the following list of organizations concerned with the issues debated in this book. The descriptions are derived from materials provided by the organizations. All have publications or information available for interested readers. The list was compiled on the date of publication of the present volume; the information provided here may change. Be aware that many organizations take several weeks or longer to respond to inquiries, so allow as much time as possible.

Alaska Wilderness League

122 C St. NW, Washington, DC 20001
(202) 544-5205 • fax: (202) 544-5197
e-mail: info@alaskawild.org
website: www.alaskawild.org

The Alaska Wilderness League is a nonprofit corporation founded in 1993 to further the protection of Alaska's public lands. It is the only Washington, DC-based environmental group devoted full-time to protecting the Arctic National Wildlife Refuge (AMWR) and other wilderness-quality lands in Alaska. Its website offers a wide range of materials related to ANWR, such as news updates, links to legislative documents, and the fact sheets, "Directional Drilling: The Latest Scheme to Develop the Arctic Refuge" and "Arctic National Wildlife Refuge: Not a Solution to High Gas Prices." The site also includes specific actions that individuals can take to participate in its conservation campaigns.

American Petroleum Institute (API)

1220 L St. NW, Washington, DC 20005-4070
(202) 682-8000
website: www.api.org

The American Petroleum Institute is the national trade association for the oil and natural gas industry. API represents producers, refiners, suppliers, pipeline operators, and marine transporters, as well as service and supply companies that support all segments of the industry. API speaks for the petroleum industry to the public, federal and state governments, and the media. The organization's website includes the report, "Off-Limits US Oil, Gas Worth $1.7 Trillion to Government: Study." Its related website, EnergyTomorrow.org, features extensive information about oil and natural gas exploration as well as a variety of news, blogs, and Twitter feeds specifically related to the Arctic National Wildlife Refuge.

Arctic Power

425 8th St. NW, Suite 540, Washington, DC   20004
(202) 248-4468 • fax: (202) 248-6123
e-mail: feedback@anwr.org
website: www.anwr.org

Arctic Power has been working since 1992 to convince politicians in the federal government to approve drilling in the Coastal Plain of the Arctic National Wildlife Refuge (ANWR). Individuals from all walks of life and professions participate as members of this nonprofit organization, supporting its mission of education and outreach to promote reasonable and safe oil development within ANWR. Arctic Power has published extensive fact sheets reporting the need and benefits of drilling in the Coastal Plain as well as outlining the pro-drilling side of the ANWR debate; all of them are available on the Arctic Power website.

Arctic Slope Regional Corporation (ASRC)

PO Box 129, Barrow, AK   99723
(800) 770-2772 • fax: (907) 852-5733
e-mail: thardt@asrc.com
website: www.asrc.com

Arctic Slope Regional Corporation was established pursuant to the Alaska Native Claims Settlement Act of 1971. ASRC is a private, for-profit corporation that is owned by and represents the business interests of eleven thousand Iñupiat Eskimo shareholders. It has been the largest locally-owned and operated business in Alaska for the past sixteen years, and its operations include oil and gas exploration and development. ASRC owns nearly five million acres of land on Alaska's North Slope that contain high potential for oil and gas production. ASRC is committed to developing these resources and bringing them to market, in a manner that respects Iñupiat subsistence values while ensuring proper care of the environment, habitat, and wildlife.

Audubon Alaska

441 W Fifth Ave., Suite 300, Anchorage, AK   99501
(907) 276-7034 • fax: (907) 276-5069
e-mail: www.audubon.org/email/1593/field_location_email
website: http://ak.audubon.org

Audubon Alaska's mission is to conserve the natural ecosystems of Alaska, focusing on birds, other wildlife, and their habitats, for the benefit and enjoyment of current and future generations of all Americans. The organization uses science to identify conservation priorities and support conservation actions and policies, with an emphasis on public lands and waters. Since its establishment in 1977, Audubon Alaska has played crucial roles in many landmark conservation victories across the state, and protecting the Arctic National Wildlife Refuge (ANWR) is one of its top priorities. The Audubon Alaska website offers a great deal of information about the birds and wildlife of ANWR, including the reports "Birds and Oil Development," "From the Arctic to Your Backyard: Arctic Birds Migrate to Your State," and a "Map of Key Arctic Wildlife Habitat."

Cato Institute

1000 Massachusetts Ave. NW, Washington, DC   20001-5403
(202) 842-0200 • fax: (202) 842-3490
website: www.cato.org

Cato Institute, a libertarian public policy organization, researches and provides policy suggestions to the government, emphasizing the values of democracy, a free market economy, and limited government. Cato analysts insist that privatizing development of the Arctic National Wildlife Refuge (ANWR) oil reserves would provide the best opportunity to utilize this natural resource, and while ANWR oil might not increase national security or reduce US energy problems, they argue that market-driven policies provide better solutions than political decisions. Cato fellows have authored reports such as "ANWR's Private Potential," "Energy Illogic," and "Don't Worry About Energy Security" providing information on these views.

Defenders of Wildlife

1130 17th St. NW, Washington, DC   20036
(800) 385-9712
e-mail: defenders@mail.defenders.org
website: www.defenders.org

Beginning with its founding in 1947, Defenders of Wildlife has worked to promote protection of wildlife and their habitats worldwide. The organization's website, Help Save the Arctic National Wildlife Refuge (www.savearcticrefuge.org), provides information detailing why drilling in the refuge should not be permitted. Additionally, publications on this site offer information about the impact of drilling on specific species, such as polar bears, caribou, and birds; facts about the oil industry and oil supplies; and expert and public opinion on the issue.

Gwich'in Steering Committee

122 First Ave., Box 2, Fairbanks, AK   99701
(907) 458-8264 • fax: (907) 457-8265
e-mail: gwichinl@alsaka.net

Founded in 1988 to combat the increasing push from the US federal government and industry to open the Coastal Plain in the Arctic National Wildlife Refuge (ANWR), the Gwich'in Steering Committee continues to promote preservation of the refuge in its natural state due to the land's cultural significance to the Gwich'in people. The committee published the report "A Moral Choice for the United States: The Human

Rights Implications for the Gwich'in of Drilling in the Arctic National Wildlife Refuge," detailing the importance of ANWR land and the wildlife that it supports.

Heritage Foundation

214 Massachusetts Ave. NE, Washington, DC   20002-4999
(202) 546-4400 • fax: (202) 546-8328
e-mail: info@heritage.org
website: www.heritage.org

The Heritage Foundation is a conservative think tank that provides information to the public and policymakers in support of conservative policies exemplifying ideals such as free enterprise, limited government, and strong national defense. As a result, on the issues of drilling in the Arctic National Wildlife Refuge (ANWR), the foundation's stance is decidedly pro-drilling, based not only on arguments of free enterprise but also on the position that utilizing oil from ANWR would reduce America's dependence on foreign oil, thus increasing national security. Reports detailing these arguments include "Opening ANWR: Long Overdue," "American-Made Energy from ANWR at a Modest Cost," and "Why Not Explore ANWR?"—all of which are available on the organization's website.

Natural Resources Defense Council (NRDC)

40 W 20th St., New York, NY   10011
(212) 727-2700 • fax: (212) 727-1773
e-mail: nrdcinfo@nrdc.org
website: www.nrdc.org

The Natural Resources Defense Council promotes international protection of wildlife and wild places through law, science, and a membership of over one million. Some of the main focuses of the organization include reduction of global temperatures, development of alternative technologies for energy, and protection of the world's oceans and endangered habitats. The NRDC has also focused its attention on protecting the Arctic National Wildlife Refuge (ANWR) from being opened for oil development and drilling, publishing detailed reports, such as "Arctic Refuge 101," as well as a video outlining the negative impact of drilling in ANWR.

Porcupine Caribou Management Board

Box 31723, Whitehorse   YT Y1A 6L3
  Canada
(867) 633-4780 • fax: (867) 393-3904
e-mail: pcmb@taiga.net
website: http://taiga.net/pcmb/index.html

The Porcupine Caribou Management Board works to manage the Porcupine caribou herd, one of the largest herds of migratory caribou on the continent, and protect and maintain its habitat. The herd faces numerous threats, including climate change and increasing human activity within its range. The herd's calving grounds lie on the Coastal Plain of the Arctic National Wildlife Refuge, which faces potential development for oil and gas exploration. The group's website offers extensive information about the Porcupine caribou herd, its migratory habitats, and the ecosystem that supports it.

Sierra Club

85 Second St., 2nd Floor, San Francisco, CA   94105
(415) 977-5500 • fax: (415) 977-5797
e-mail: information@sierraclub.org
website: www.sierraclub.org

The Sierra Club, an environmental protection organization founded in 1892, works to ensure the conservation of natural habitats, preservation of species, and caretaking of the planet as a whole. The organization focuses much of its effort on combating global warming through innovative energy technologies and preserving American wilderness through public education and outreach. Sierra Club also dedicates a section of its website to explaining the reasons why drilling in the Arctic National Wildlife Refuge (ANWR) should not be permitted and providing opportunities for individuals to become involved in the campaign against opening the ANWR.

US Department of the Interior (DOI)

1849 C St. NW, Washington, DC   20240
(202) 208-3100
e-mail: feedback@ios.doi.gov
website: www.doi.gov

The US Department of the Interior is the federal government agency dedicated to protecting America's natural lands and resources and the accompanying recreational opportunities. The organization works closely with native people across America to ensure their rights to the land are protected. DOI has been performing these duties since its creation in 1849. With regards to the Arctic National Wildlife Refuge(ANWR), the agency's position has been to promote responsible, environmentally sound drilling and development in order to fully utilize the natural oil reserves present in the Coastal Plain area. The DOI website offers fact sheets and reports detailing the impact of drilling on ANWR as well as the positive effects on the economy and national security.

US Senate Committee on Energy and Natural Resources

304 Dirksen Senate Building, Washington, DC   20510
(202) 224-4971 • fax: (202) 224-6163
e-mail: www.energy.senate.gov/public/index.cfm/contact
website: www.energy.senate.gov

The US Senate Committee on Energy and Natural Resources is the senatorial body that has jurisdiction over matters related to energy and public lands. Its far-reaching legislative activity covers energy resources and development, regulation and conservation, strategic petroleum reserves, public lands and their renewable resources, surface mining, federal coal, oil and gas, other mineral leasing, and water resources. Full transcripts for testimony related to the Arctic National Wildlife Refuge are archived on the committee's website.

Bibliography

Books

Dean Baker
Hot Air over the Arctic: An Assessment of the WEFA Study of the Economic Impact of Oil Drilling in the Arctic National Wildlife Refuge. Washington, DC: Center for Economic Policy and Research, 2001.

Subhankar Banerjee
Arctic National Wildlife Refuge: Seasons of Life and Land. Seattle, WA: Mountaineers Books, 2003.

Rick Bass
Caribou Rising: Defending the Porcupine Herd, Gwich'in Culture, and the Arctic National Wildlife Refuge. San Francisco, CA: Sierra Club Books, 2004.

Sarah Billingshouse
Arctic National Wildlife Refuge Issues and Legislation. Hauppauge, NY: Nova Science Publishers, 2009.

M. Lynne Corn
Arctic National Wildlife Refuge: Background and Issues. Hauppauge, NY: Nova Science Publishers, 2003.

Michael Farrar
A Line in the Snow: The Battle for ANWR, the Arctic National Wildlife Refuge. Bloomington, IN: iUniverse, 2009.

Richard Fineberg   *Understanding the US Geological Survey Analysis of Estimated Oil Beneath the Coastal Plain of the Arctic National Wildlife Refuge.* Fairbanks, AK: Research Associates, 2001.

Robert Fischman   *The National Wildlife Refuges: Coordinating a Conservation System Through Law.* Washington, DC: Island Press, 2003.

Matthew Kotchen and Nicholas Burger   *Should We Drill in the Arctic National Wildlife Refuge? An Economic Perspective, NBER Working Paper No. 13211.* Boston, MA: National Bureau of Economic Research, Inc., 2007.

Barbara Lieland   *Arctic National Wildlife Refuge (ANWR): Review, Controversies and Legislation.* London, United Kingdom: Gazelle Distribution, 2006.

Ken Madsen   *Under the Arctic Sun: Gwich'in, Caribou, and the Arctic National Wildlife Refuge.* Watsonville, CA: Earthtales Press, 2003.

David Robinson   *Oil Beneath Our Feet: America's Energy Non-Crisis.* Seattle, WA: CreateSpace, 2010.

Bruce Smith   *Where Elk Roam: Conservation and Biopolitics of Our National Elk Herd.* Guilford, CT: Lyons Press, 2011.

US Fish and Wildlife Service — *Arctic National Wildlife Refuge: Final Comprehensive Conservation Plan, Environmental Impact Statement, Wilderness Review, and Wild River Plans.* Washington, DC: US Government Printing Office, 2011.

Jonathan Waterman — *Where Mountains Are Nameless: Passion and Politics in the Arctic National Wildlife Refuge.* New York: W.W. Norton and Company, 2007.

Periodicals and Internet Sources

Alaska Journal of Commerce — "House Approves Opening ANWR—Again," February 16, 2012. www.alaskajournal.com.

Audubon Alaska — "Birds and Oil Development in the Arctic Refuge," 2001. www.ak.audubon.org.

John Balzar — "Down the Hulahula: The Arctic National Wildlife Refuge Is Wilderness Without Qualification. The Question Is, Should It Stay that Way?" *Los Angeles Times*, June 20, 1993.

Felicity Barringer — "A Quest for Oil Collides with Nature in Alaska," *New York Times*, October 2, 2005.

Cutler Cleveland and Robert Kaufmann — "Oil Supply and Oil Politics: Deja Vu All Over Again," *Energy Policy*, vol. 31, no. 6, pp. 485–89, May 2003.

Bernard A. Gelb   "ANWR Development: Economic Impacts," Congressional Research Service, January 24, 2006. www.crs.ncseonline.org.

Gwich'in Steering Committee   "A Moral Choice for the United States: The Human Rights Implications for the Gwich'in of Drilling in the Arctic National Wildlife Refuge," 2005.

Dave Harbour   "Crude Realities—Let Alaska Jumpstart Economy," *Richmond Times Dispatch*, August 5, 2009.

Steve Hargreaves   "The Oil Industry's Plan to Lower Gas Prices," *CNN Money*, March 23, 2012. http://money.cnn.com.

Doc Hastings   "Forget 10 Years—Drilling ANWR Would Pay Off Right Away," *US News & World Report*, November 3, 2011.

M. Herndon   "The Last Frontier," *Forum for Applied Research and Public Policy*, vol. 16, no. 4, p. 72, 2002.

Phil Izzo   "Don't Expect Too Much from ANWR," *Wall Street Journal*, June 18, 2008. http://blogs.wsj.com.

Deborah Jacobs   "The Caribou Question and Alaskan Oil," *PERC Reports*, vol. 19, no. 2, Summer 2001.

Nash Keune   "ANWR, Our Frozen Energy Debate:
                        No Better Time to End the
                        Arguments About Drilling in Alaska,"
                        National Review Online, February 23,
                        2012. www.nationalreview.com.

Tim Korte   "Groups Argue Western Areas Are
                        'Too Wild to Drill'," *Los Angeles
                        Times*, August 3, 2008.
                        www.articles.latimes.com.

Daniel Lashof et   "Oil from the Arctic National
al.   Wildlife Refuge: Too Little, Too Late,"
                        Natural Resources Defense Council,
                        2001. www.nrdc.org.

Armory and   "Fool's Gold in Alaska," *Foreign
Hunter Lovins   Affairs*, July–August 2001.

Natural Resources   "Fuelish Claims—Drilling the Arctic
Defense Council   Won't Create a Significant Number
                        of Jobs," 2001. www.nrdc.org.

Irven Palmer Jr.   "Why ANWR? Is There Really Any
                        Oil There?" *Alaska Business Monthly*,
                        April 6, 2011.

PBS NewsHour   "The ANWR Drilling Debate,"
                        November 2, 2005. www.pbs.org.

Lydia Saad   "U.S. Oil Drilling Gains Favor with
                        Americans—Support for Offshore
                        Drilling and Oil Exploration in
                        Alaska Reach New Highs,"
                        Gallup.com, March 14, 2011.
                        www.gallup.com.

Elizabeth Shogren   "For 30 Years, a Political Battle over
                     Oil and ANWR," *All Things
                     Considered,* November 10, 2005.
                     www.npr.org.

Ben Spiess   "Arctic Oil Drilling Debate Escalates,"
                     Anchorage Daily News, May 7, 2001.

The Toledo Blade   "All of the Above," March 23, 2012.

US Fish and   "Potential Impacts of Proposed Oil
Wildlife Service   and Gas Development on the Arctic
                     Refuge's Coastal Plain: Historical
                     Overview and Issues of Concern,"
                     January 2001. http://arctic.fws.gov.

US Geological   "Oil and Gas Potential of the Arctic
Survey   National Wildlife Refuge 1002 Area,
                     Alaska," US Department of the
                     Interior, Open File Report 98–34,
                     1999. http://pubs.usgs.gov.

Index

A

Alaback, Paul, 33–39
Alaska Department of Environmental Conservation, 89, 92
Alaska National Interest Lands Conservation Act (ANILCA), 59, 61, 63, 82
Alaska National Petroleum Reserve, 44–45
Alaska Native Claims Settlement Act (ANCSA), 59
Alaska Oil & Gas Association, 42
Alaska Oil and Gas Conservation Commission, 91
Alaskan Energy for American Jobs Act, 60, 61, 62, 65
Alyeska Pipeline, 42, 44
Andrews Air Force Base, 72
Annual Energy Outlook Reference Case, 22
Anti-drilling factions, 16
Anti-hydrocarbon policies, 17
Arctic Grayling (fish), 35
Arctic National Wildlife Refuge (ANWR)
    Area 10-02, 82–83
    caribou calving grounds impact, 35–36
    caribou herd compatible with drilling, 53–57
    caribou herd shrinkage from drilling in, 47–52
    as climate change resource, 37–38
    Coastal Plain, 7–8, 23, 54

    development as beneficial, 56–57
    disruptive ecological changes, 37
    drilling as insignificant in, 81–86
    environmental stewardship of, 84–85
    fact-finding mission to, 83–84
    geologic background, 22
    historic preservation opportunity, 38–39
    holds oil potential, 11–19
    major oil spill in, 87–93
    mission of, 34–35
    oil production delay, 40–46
    overview, 7–10, 14–15
    protect from drilling, 33–39
    See also Drilling
Arctic Power group, 83
Arctic Slope Regional Corporation (ASRC), 59–60, 63
Arctic wolves, 31, 35
Argentina, 41

B

Bachman, Michele, 42
Bathurst caribou herd, 51
Beaufort Sea, 29, 34, 38, 44
Beaufort Sea bears, 36
Belden Russonello & Stewart, 30
Bering Sea, 44
Big Oil, 29–31
Biodiesel, 24
Biofuel mandate, 26–27
BP Oil, 42, 84, 88–92
Brazil, 12, 41, 45